Underdevelopment

The process of globalization, evidenced by environmental change, migration, industrial relations and the extraordinary acceleration of industrial economic relations, has not led to increased convergence in the global economy. Rather, in some cases it has been accompanied by greater divergence between the fortunes of the world's richest and poorest nations. Professor Sylos Labini argues that mainstream economics provides limited help in considering these phenomena and instead adopts the perspectives of Adam Smith, David Ricardo and Thomas Robert Malthus, who put economic growth at the centre of their analyses.

In this short book he offers a new approach to the theory of economic growth and reminds us of the great variety of economic trajectories in developing countries. He further proposes a strategy of institutional reform to respond to the problem of underdevelopment. For Africa, he recommends a strategy of organizational reforms, including a programme to eradicate illiteracy and to promote rural and industrial districts.

Paolo Sylos Labini is Professor Emeritus at the University of Rome. He has made many important contributions to the field of economics and economic theory. Some of his recent publications include *The Forces of Economic Growth and Decline* (1984) and *Economic Growth and Business Cycles – Prices and the Process of Cyclical Development* (1993) as well as many journal articles.

Federico Caffè Lectures

This series of annual lectures was initiated to honour the memory of Federico Caffè. They are jointly sponsored by the Department of Public Economics at the University of Rome, where Caffè held a chair from 1959 to 1987, and the Bank of Italy, where he served for many years as an adviser. The publication of the lectures will provide a vehicle for leading scholars in the economics profession, and for the interested general reader, to reflect on the pressing economic and social issues of the times.

Underdevelopment

A Strategy for Reform

Paolo Sylos Labini

CAMBRIDGE
UNIVERSITY PRESS

PUBLISHED BY THE PRESS SYNDICATE OF THE UNIVERSITY OF CAMBRIDGE
The Pitt Building, Trumpington Street, Cambridge, United Kingdom

CAMBRIDGE UNIVERSITY PRESS
The Edinburgh Building, Cambridge CB2 2RU, UK
40 West 20th Street, New York, NY 10011-4211, USA
10 Stamford Road, Oakleigh, VIC 3166, Australia
Ruiz de Alarcón 13, 28014 Madrid, Spain
Dock House, The Waterfront, Cape Town 8001, South Africa

http://www.cambridge.org

First published 2001

Printed in the United Kingdom at the University Press, Cambridge

Typeface Melior 10/13   *System* QuarkXPress™   [SE]

A catalogue record for this book is available from the British Library

Library of Congress Cataloguing in Publication data

Sylos Labini, Paolo.
Underdevelopment : a strategy for reform / Paolo Sylos Labini.
    p.   cm. – (Frederico Caffè lectures)
Includes bibliographical references and index.
ISBN 0-521-58869-3
1. Developing countries–Economic policy. 2. Developing
countries–Economic conditions. 3. Developing countries–Social policy.
4. Economic development. 5. Institution building. 6. Africa–Economic
policy. 7. Africa–Social policy. I. Title. II. Series.
HC59.7 .S898 2001
338.9′009172′4–dc21   00-045553

ISBN 0 521 58869 3 hardback

Contents

Figures and tables

Figures

Tables

Introduction

Underdevelopment and the methodological approach of Adam Smith

After the beginning of the process of decolonization, at the conclusion of the Second World War, several economists began to study systematically the problems of underdeveloped countries. These problems were considered from both the analytical and the practical standpoint – that is, with the purpose of understanding the causes of underdevelopment and of suggesting measures of economic policy intended to promote growth. A number of recommendations emerged from this work – some of which were mutually exclusive, others complementary; some of limited, others of great relevance. Economists advocated measures to promote import substitution (with protection) or to increase exports, particularly of labour-intensive manufactured goods; measures to stimulate an increase in aggregate savings as a prerequisite of investment; the speeding up of investment in human capital and particularly in education; and, more recently, elimination of the obstacles to international trade and to domestic markets for products and labour and privatization of the productive activities carried out by the state through public enterprises.

The latter recommendation has acquired new vigour after the epoch-making failure of central planning, made evident by the breakdown of the Soviet Union. At different periods the Soviet Union itself supported certain underdeveloped countries, attempting to introduce in them, if not a proper system of central planning, at least a system of tight regulation of prices and production. Some economists, following Marx, recommended the expropriation of the means of production to introduce a system of central planning. At the same time others suggested entering, via changes in international alliances or a revolution, the area of influence of the Soviet Union, after breaking ties with the United States: in their view, the latter, being an imperialist power, represented the main obstacle to the development of backward countries.

Putting aside the revolutionary perspective, which has failed dramatically, we can see that some of the specific aforementioned recommendations have proved to be wrong, whereas others have been applied with more positive results.

However, to overcome underdevelopment, I think that economists have to give less attention to measures of economic policy and to devote much greater intellectual efforts to the problem of institutional and organizational reforms, that require time both to be prepared and (even more so, to be carried out: there are no short cuts). The very results of different measures of economic policy are conditioned by the gradual implementation of reforms. Some organizational changes can be introduced in public administration by political leaders without new laws; changes in the organization of economic units can be introduced by entrepreneurs. Other changes, particularly institutional ones, can be introduced by means only of new laws. Such changes must occur relatively frequently, since the framework in which the market for goods, services and labour operates does not remain static, even in the short run. Changes in the legal framework are particularly important owing to their general influence: however, it is one thing when such changes are introduced piecemeal, under the pressure of specific problems, and a completely different thing when they are introduced according to a strategy. This is especially true in the case of underdeveloped countries that try to start or to speed up their process of economic growth. To be sure, working out such institutional and organizational reforms is the task of experts in public and private law. But economists should work hand in hand with jurists to advise on the measures best capable of promoting growth. The advice of political scientists and of sociologists is also necessary. It can be direct but also indirect – that is, as Keynes put it, by means of 'pamphlets thrown to the wind'. Such advice is necessary, since reforms are not simply an intellectual affair: they affect the cultural values and economic and non-economic interests of social classes. Thus politicians would do well not to simply trust their intuition, but should listen to social scientists to try and reduce the risk of serious mistakes.

The reflections were the origin of a book published in Italian in 1983 and in Spanish two years later (Sylos Labini, 1983a). Some of these views were discussed in a review article written by my friend Federico Caffè (Caffè, 1983). Subsequently the Bank of Italy, of which he was advisor for many years, to honour his memory decided to promote every year some special lectures, by inviting contributions from both foreign and Italian economists. Among the former, Edmund Malinvaud, Robert Solow and János Kornai were invited; among the latter, Luigi Pasinetti, Augusto Graziani and myself. This book derives from the the lectures that I delivered in April 1993 in the Department of Economics of the University of Rome, where Federico Caffè taught for many years. However, those lectures were only the starting point: given the importance and the complexity of the question, I was motivated to work out afresh and develop the whole analysis.

The approach that I adopt here owes much to Adam Smith's *Wealth of Nations*. In examining the conditions for economic growth, Smith had studied the historical evolution of a number of countries, especially but not exclusively European ones. For Smith, historical inquiry was the necessary basis for the theoretical analysis of economic processes. At the end of his analyses, Smith advocated several fundamental reforms. Of these, I will mention only five: (1) the abolition of the exclusive privileges and, more generally, of all the fetters to markets left as a legacy of the feudal system; (2) the reform of the property rights over land to make easier its mobility, both in heredity transfers and in the market – in Smith's times the persistence of feudal legal institutions were still creating serious obstacles to both types of mobility; (3) the reform of agricultural contracts; (4) a fiscal reform, to be based on four 'maxims' concerning taxes (equality, certainty, convenience of payment, economy of collection) and (5) the reform of the institutions of education.

Economists all over the world retain a great respect for Adam Smith, considered the founder of our science, which for him concerned primarily the economic development of nations. Yet, most of my colleagues do not believe that it is worth studying his *Wealth of Nations* – not to mention his *Theory of Moral Sentiments* and his *Lectures on Jurisprudence* – since for them such a study is not important to interpret the economic problems of our own time. In their judgement, having put aside the historical analysis, what is scientifically of worth in the Smithian theoretical apparatus has by now been absorbed in modern theoretical models. This view is misguided, especially in the case of the growth of underdeveloped countries, in which the institutional framework cannot be taken for granted, although this, but only as a first approximation, can be done in the case of developed countries. Today the influence of Adam Smith in the analysis of development is very limited indeed: the economists who have absorbed and made use of his lessons are very few. Few, however, but excellent: Arthur Lewis, Amartya Sen, Giorgio Fuà and Paul Streeten, whose works are entirely in the spirit of Smith.

From Smith we can appreciate not only the conceptual importance of unifying problems belonging to different fields of research (economic history, economic theory, demography, political science) to overcome the damaging – at times even schizophrenic – consequences of the extreme division of labour that often prevails in the analysis of societies. We can also learn that, to try and interpret the economic evolution of different societies, we have to consider together three fundamental aspects: culture, institutions and natural resources.

Resources, including climate, land, forests, mines, seas and rivers, plus geographical position, condition the economic evolution of the developing countries. Yet, the abundance of certain resources has had different consequences in different countries: in some, at least in the first stage of their evolution, it performed a positive role in the growth of national wealth; in others it was the source of enormous wealth for tiny minorities while the great majority of the people remained in a state of poverty (consider, for instance, certain oil-producing Arabian countries). On the other hand, countries endowed with scarce resources have been capable of starting and sustaining a process of growth with relatively low inequality in income distribution. These contrasted results bring out very clearly the fundamental relevance of the other two factors – culture and institutions – which are to a large extent interlocked: after all, the institutions themselves are a product of culture.

'Culture' is intended in a broad sense. It must include the philosophical views prevailing in the country considered and the daily philosophy of the common people, and religion (certain religions, at least as they were practised in given historical periods, are favourable, others are utterly unhelpful to modern economic growth). Of course, culture includes also the organization of education and of scientific research; finally, it encompasses literature, music, arts and human and experimental sciences.

The wealth of the few and the poverty of the many

The most serious cases of backwardness and mass poverty can be found in a number of African – and, to a lesser extent, in Asian – countries that until relatively recently were colonies of European countries or were controlled by them or by the United States. In all cases the rulers were white people.

In the nineteenth century there was a widespread rhetoric of a 'White Man's burden', intended to emphasize the positive effects exerted by the colonizers – who, being in many senses more advanced, had the historical duty to help the progress of the natives. In recent times this optimistic rhetoric has often been replaced by a rhetoric of the opposite type, according to which many of the backward countries are poor because they have been cheated of important shares of their resources – an international redistribution of world resources and the exploitation of the stronger are the origin of the riches of the few and the poverty of the many. This latter conception has been and still is popular in certain sectors of the Catholic Church and among Marxian intellectuals.

Both conceptions are wrong. The abuses committed by the Europeans should by no means be belittled. The slave trade that lasted for more than two centuries involved many millions of human beings. The massacres of natives in North and South America, the forced transformation of independent workers, often members of tribes, into wage earners in several African regions, the expropriation of large areas, after the expulsion of the natives, to organize plantations or mines or create towns are only a few of the most egregious misdeeds. Yet, before the conquest of the Europeans in primitive communities life was by no means idyllic. Ethnic conflicts, tribal wars and predatory incursions were the rule, with the consequent degradation and enslavement of the losers. Moreover, during the slave trade white merchants were often fetching negroes on the coasts who had been captured in the interior and sold to them by other negroes. In fact, the characteristic

feature of the tragedy of man has been that stronger populations have tended to overwhelm weaker, either through wars
or by corrupting their leaders. This has occurred for very different reasons: to make the subjugated people the conqueror's
slaves, not necessarily for economic advantage; to exterminate the inhabitants of certain territories in order to seize
their land; to exterminate masses of people, simply out of
hatred, or to carry out an 'ethnic cleansing'. In all this, the
economic motives often are not the most important ones.

Is then Hobbes right in his motto, '*homo homini lupus*'?
Certainly, he is not wrong. But the picture is not wholly
black. I agree with the observations made by Smith with reference to the countries transformed into colonies:

> At the particular time when these [geographic] discoveries were
> made, the superiority of force happened to be so great on the side
> of the Europeans, that they were unable to commit with impu-
> nity every sort of injustice in those remote countries. Hereafter,
> perhaps, the natives of those countries may grow stronger, or
> those of Europe may grow weaker, and the inhabitants of all the
> different quarters of the world may arrive at that equality of
> courage and force which, by inspiring mutual fear, can alone
> overawe the injustice of independent nations into some sort of
> respect for the rights of one another. But nothing seems to be
> more likely to establish this equality of force than that mutual
> communication of knowledge and of all sort of improvements
> which an extensive commerce from all countries to all countries
> naturally, or rather necessarily, carries along with it. (Smith, 1961
> [1776], book IV, ch. VII, part III)

No doubt, independence is the prerequisite for economic
and civic development. Five centuries after those discoveries
Smith's hopes have been realized in only a few countries.
Often independence has been formal, or it has been real to
only a limited extent. The road to be travelled is very difficult, but it is not entirely blocked. In certain countries, especially in South East Asia, certain intellectuals, educated in
Europe, embraced the ideas of European revolutionaries to

pursue independence by breaking any tie with capitalism. Their efforts have caused death and suffering on a large scale without significant progress on the road to civilization. However, even the tragic experiences that we have witnessed show that culture counts, for bad – as we have seen in several cases – or for good – as we have seen in others: history sometimes can teach us something.

Going back to the strict economic standpoint, it is wrong to believe that the wealth of the few and the poverty of the many depend mainly on the exploitation imposed by force and violence by the developed countries on the underdeveloped. The sharp contrast depends primarily on the different cultural evolution of the two categories of countries. The exploitation of the more powerful countries, that as a rule concerns agricultural and mineral raw materials, has played a collateral role: one can speak of exploitation owing to the ways, hinted at above, that the dominant countries have adopted to get hold of those raw materials. When such materials are obtained through the usual commercial channels, as well as when they are sold by developed countries, we cannot properly speak of 'exploitation'. The responsibilities of the white colonizers are much more serious in destroying the cultural and organizational traditions of local communities, in creating totally artificial nations and, as we will see in chapter 6, in breaking down the demographic equilibrium without promoting but, on the contrary, hindering economic growth.

A cultural break point at the dawn of economic and civic development

A striking feature of many underdeveloped countries is the coexistence of traditional and modern components. Thus in areas of Africa and Asia we find human groups that still are in a stage of development that in present-day advanced societies could be found centuries or even thousands of years ago. When culture is stagnating, the whole social life and the way of living and of producing the means necessary to survive do not change, or change only marginally. Without a break point underdevelopment – both cultural and economic – can go on indefinitely. In the Middle East, in North Africa and in Europe such a break point took place at least four thousand years ago and it was a radical break, whose reasons are far from clear. It seems that in other parts of the world similar breaks took place, but they were not so old and deep. Under the influence of a process of world unification, that today is undergoing an ever more intense acceleration but started long ago, at least after the great geographic discoveries, the routine of underdevelopment has in an increasing number of areas been broken. However, after the break, often imposed from outside, the process that has been called 'modernization' appears to be slow and painful.

Culture develops only in societies where, given a non-negligible basis of education, political freedom prevails. In such conditions, ideas and interests conflicting with those of the rulers are not strangled by repression, and tolerance as well as persuasion – the Greek goddess Πειθώ, praised by Plato (in Latin, Suadela) – constitute the fundamental rules of behaviour. In societies in which political freedom is restricted, culture in general and scientific culture in particular show very slow progress, as recent experiences have demonstrated. In the long run, economic growth itself depends on the growth of culture, which conditions not only technological but also organizational and institutional innovation. Today the economy of the largest country in the world, China, is growing very fast. This growth can go on as long as it can profit from already existing technologies and adaptations or improvements embodied in machinery and equipment imported from advanced countries, where cultural growth is strong and political freedom is the rule. In the long run, however, if such freedom is not admitted, economic development is bound to slow down since such development is conditioned by scientific progress that, without freedom, cannot but be imitative and weak.

The market as an institutional framework originated by a long evolution

From the economic standpoint the market, which in reality presents very different configurations, is the most important of all institutions. Many contemporary economists reason as if the market were a natural – an eternal – institution, a view only recently and for only a few decades challenged by the experience of centrally planned economies. The fact that their experience broke down in failure has reinforced this conviction. But it is not true that the market is a natural phenomenon: it is the product of a secular evolution and has undergone deep changes in the course of time. The market, before appearing as an economic phenomenon, presents itself as a legal framework. The truth is that the market is not an open field and the laissez-faire policy, taken literally, is meaningless. We should say instead, '*le marché c'est la loi*': law creates the institutional embankments between which the waters of the economy can flow. Without them, water becomes marsh or generates floods. Laws can be enacted wisely or wrongly; they can fix automatic rules or leave to bureaucracies a dangerous discretionary power; they can be simple and rational or dreadfully complicated and restrictive. But laws are necessary.

The market is certainly a most powerful engine of growth. But, if it is wrong to belittle its great potentialities, it is also wrong to extol its virtues; laws have to take full account of its faults. The market works very well in the case of standardized commodities, less well with differentiated commodities. Serious problems arise with services, especially highly sophisticated services, like those of doctors and surgeons. Special problems arise in the case of the environment. Finally, we have to keep monopolistic markets well separated from those in which competitive firms incessantly introduce innovations to outdo each other.

The market did not exist in primitive societies and even today exists in limited areas, in societies that retain many features of what today we call 'backwardness' and that long ago prevailed everywhere. Thus, in certain Asian and in several African countries village communities are still relevant; in Russia, until the Bolshevik revolution, the peasants' communities (*Mir*) had an important economic and social role. The appearance of the product market preceded the appearance of the labour market, which differs very much from the former, today even more than in the past. Today an index of the degree of social development of a number of underdeveloped societies is given by the share of dependent workers in the labour force. Even the label 'independent workers' has different meanings in primitive societies from that which it has acquired in advanced societies. Moreover, in primitive societies self-consumption is important, so that statistical data concerning production, especially agriculture, tend to underestimate quantities. Basically, in traditional societies relations among individuals are personal, whereas in advanced societies they are often impersonal – the 'cash nexus' prevails. However, even in such societies we find organizational forms that, though conditioned by the market, do not belong to the proper market area – non-profit institutions, for example, and cooperatives.

In its historical evolution the market has changed its role: in addition of working as a value-meter, in the epoch of industrial capitalism the institutions constituting the market have been gradually enlarged to favour technological and organizational innovations of firms – that is, to strengthen dynamic competition, that goes much beyond the small variations converging towards equilibrium prices and brings about, via productivity increases, either systematic cost and price reductions or rising money incomes and in any case an incessant flow of new goods.

The neoclassical paradigm and the theory of development

The neoclassical theory is still the dominant paradigm in economics. Until recently it was static, in the sense that neoclassical economists were considering curves expressing a series of hypothetical variations, outside the real time, given techniques of production. Thus neoclassical theory could not be used to analyse the process of growth, nor, in particular, technical progress – a very paradoxical situation, if we recognize that we are living in a period in which economic and social relations are unceasingly revolutionized by great innovations accompanied and followed by all sorts of minor innovations. A group of economists have attempted to modify this state of affairs, trying to introduce technical progress and growth in their models, without abandoning the neoclassical framework. I will briefly discuss critically such attempts in chapter 4 (pp. 91–5).

The neoclassical models have their matrix in Walrasian general equilibrium theory. The situation is different with Keynesian theory: the original model is static, but in certain aspects proved to be amenable to dynamic developments. In fact, certain fundamental Keynesian functions can be used, without manipulation, in a dynamic analysis. This is the case with the savings and the consumption functions, which are represented by curves that we can interpret either as syntheses of hypothetical variations or as variations occurring in real time. Harrod (1942) and Domar (1957) make use of the savings function in their growth models, which can be considered as Keynesian; they are certainly dynamic, since they apply to variations occurring at different points of time, although they allow for technical progress only implicitly. Other models, compatible with Keynesian theory, can well be considered as dynamic. Milton Friedman's model of the consumption function as well as Franco Modigliani's model of the life cycle belong to this category. In all these models, however, the process of growth is assumed but not explained. Moreover, technical and organizational progress is seen as an exogenous variable: no importance is attributed to the fact that it affects the various economic activities in different ways. Since technical and organizational progress is, by its very nature, an unbalanced process, it seems that only multi-sectoral models can allow us properly to take it into account; this is not possible if we adopt one-sector models. On the other hand, the explanation of the growth process is bound to be inadequate if we do not attempt to specify and explain the impulses generating the growth of productivity. Such problems will be discussed in chapters 3 and 4, where I propose a critique of the main pillars of mainstream economics and where I try to work out the thesis that no analytical separation should be admitted between the growth models related to advanced and those relating to underdeveloped countries.

The number of models adopting the multi-sectoral approach is still extremely limited, but an awareness that a change in the paradigm is necessary seems to be spreading, so that we can be very cautiously optimistic for the future. Pareto criticized the old economists because they were reasoning in terms of cause-and-effect relations whereas, for him, the approach to be adopted was that of general equilibrium, based on the concept of interdependence at a given point of time. Today, having recognized the sterility of such models for interpreting the economic processes that matter most, we have to substitute the criterion of interdependence by that of the interaction among variables that have a necessary time dimension – a criterion, it must be added, more akin to that of the classical than to that of most of the contemporary economists. An important analytical tool to be used, in both the theoretical models and in empirical research, is rates of change in the course of time of the phenomena being studied. After all, in spite of the scepticism of many economists, econometric models, if worked out on adequate theoretical foundations, can represent important steps in the right direction.

'Growth economics', a label covering several models worked out after the Second World War by a number of brilliant economists, remained separate from the main body of economic theory, that was and to a large extent still is essentially static. Not only time but, as Paul Krugman emphasizes, space too (localization problems) has remained absent from mainstream economics, probably because, as Krugman (1991) remarks, mainstream economists attribute paramount importance to mathematical formalization and are not willing to think about what they are unable to formalize. Yet, mathematics is not an end in itself: it is to be used only when it is necessary; we cannot sacrifice relevance for the sake of mathematical expressions, although our ambition should be to have both, rigour – that often but not always coincides with mathematics – and relevance.

In discussing the ways to overcome underdevelopment modern economists have concentrated their studies on measures of economic policy. The fact is that mainstream economics takes for granted the institutional and legal framework: changes of this framework should be the concern of politicians, political scientists and jurists, not of economists – a conception diametrically opposed to that of Adam Smith. The question of measures of economic policy is certainly important but, for underdeveloped countries, the question of reforms is even more important. In this book I fully adopt the Smithian point of view.

I wish to express my thanks to my colleagues and friends Enzo Grilli, Paolo Palazzi, Alessandro Roncaglia and Michele Salvati, who took the trouble of reading the preliminary draft of this book and giving me several suggestions. I express my thanks also to Luigi Pasinetti, who read and commented on chapters 3 and 4 on mainstream economics, to Umberto Colombo, who commented on the environmental

problems considered in chapter 8 and to Bruna Ingrao and
Mario Cresta, who commented on chapters 8 and 9 and on
chapter 9 and the conclusion, respectively. Bruna Ingrao,
besides being an expert of international repute in the field
of general equilibrium theory, knows the economy of
Mozambique very well – she has given several courses in the
University of Maputo; Mario Cresta is an expert in nutrition
and knows certain African countries very well, especially the
Francophone countries of Western and Equatorial Africa.

My special thanks are owed to an anonymous referee
whom – a rare occurrence – I have found in sympathy with
my approach: besides certain helpful critical comments, he
gave very useful suggestions on the order of presentation.

Some of the above-mentioned friends have pointed out to me
that my treatment of the new growth models, presented in
chapter 4 (pp. 91–5), is too short and the critical appraisal
expounded there too concise with respect to the size of this
literature. I wish to make clear to my friends and to the readers
of the book that my brevity is deliberate and is not due simply
to the fact that a systematic discussion of the new growth
models would not have been possible in a monograph such as
the present one. The main reason lies in my radical disagree-
ment with the theoretical foundations of these models that, in
spite of their assumptions, remain static and technical
progress practically exogenous. In truth, the increase of productivity, that is the main effect of technical progress, can be
seen as an endogenous variable only if it is explained by
impulses arising within the economic system. I do not see this
kind of explanation in the case of the new growth models,
which, on the other hand, attribute a key role to a production
function of the Cobb–Douglas type that, among other things,
assumes that aggregate capital can be measured independently of its returns, a logically untenable assumption. The
conception of productivity increases and the aggregate production function are two of the seven foundations of the still

dominant theoretical paradigm that I criticize in chapters 3 and 4.

A paradigm is like a pair of spectacles: if it is wrong we see an altered reality. Since I am convinced that traditional theory is misleading, I decided not to use this type of spectacles. This is why I have devoted so little space to critical comments on the new growth models. In my own analysis, I prefer to go back to the approaches of the classical economists.

Those readers who are interested in the recent contributions on growth analysis will find the relevant literature discussed in various important books and articles. For the benefit of readers who are not disturbed by the criticisms of the traditional theory raised by me and by other economists, in addition to those briefly considered in chapter 4 I can mention three recent works: Anghion and Howitt (1998); Temple (1999); and Zagler (1999).

1

Economic development in a secular perspective

The long preparation

Economic development has become a systematic process only in the last 500 years; it has become systematic and vigorous only in the last 200 years, with the development of modern industry.

The development process started in certain European countries and only later in other continents. Previously expansions of production were occurring irregularly and in limited areas, sometimes linked to migrations or wars. Technological and organizational innovations took place very irregularly. Organizational innovations took the form of new systems of legal rules applying to the behaviour of the members of a given society in their life and in their economic activities. Greece excelled in the creation of new systems of thought, that subsequently became the matrixes of modern science. Rome excelled in the creation of new rules of behaviour and new institutions, that proved to be so vital that, even after the extraordinary changes that have occurred in social and economic life in the course of centuries, they still survive to a non-negligible extent in contemporary societies – property laws, credit and debt relations, the system of contracts, laws about commerce and the organization of productive units, for example.

Technological changes applied to production became less and less rare in the last 400–500 years, hand in hand with the development of experimental science. Indeed, the relations between science and economic activity began to become systematic, starting with the epoch of the great geographic discoveries. 'The discovery of the Western Hemisphere represents the most solemn deed with which science has invaded the public economy' (Cattaneo, 1956), a discovery, we may add, that was prepared by a kind of cooperation between Christopher Columbus and Paolo Toscanelli, a fascinating thinker – great mathematician, great astronomer, great geographer: in fact, the discovery of America was, first of all, an extraordinary scientific discovery. Adam Smith put forth, and forcefully so, a similar view.

The date of the discovery of America has thus been proposed as the beginning of the modern epoch that is characterized by the rapid development of towns, as both Smith and Cattaneo have emphasized (Smith, 1961, book III, chs. III and IV; Cattaneo, 1956). In particular, they conceive the development of towns – that is, of the bourgeoisie – and that of modern scientific thought as one and the same thing.

Modern capitalism is the outcome of such developments. However, many economists speak of 'capitalism' as if it were a social system relatively stable in the course of time and relatively similar in the different countries of the world. This is not so. There is not much in common between the commercial capitalism prevailing in several European countries and in certain Asian countries in the fifteenth, sixteenth and seventeenth centuries and modern industrial capitalism. The market itself, that has been seen as the main characteristic of capitalism, is not the same, in space or time, since it does not work in a vacuum, but in a complex institutional framework that evolves over the course of time.

Three stages in the evolution of modern capitalism

During the epoch of commercial capitalism certain institutional and organizational innovations had a key role: in the commerce with colonies and in banking, the introduction of joint-stock companies with limited liability was critical; in agriculture, new types of property rights and new contracts capable of stimulating production were vitally important. During commercial capitalism technological innovations were rare; they became frequent and important during modern industrial capitalism, whose evolution took place through different stages.

The first stage is the one analysed by Adam Smith and covers the seventeenth and a good part of the eighteenth century. During this period we observe an acceleration in organizational changes in agriculture: the remnants of the feudal system were gradually eliminated, the communal forms of production were reduced to the minimum and those based on private property became dominant. During this period, in which handicraft intertwines with agriculture, industry started its development as manufacturing, to be intended in its ethimological sense (handmade). Both in agriculture and in manufacturing, innovations in the methods of production were more and more frequent, but the factory system and modern machinery were still to come.

Towards the end of the eighteenth and the beginning of the nineteenth century the Industrial Revolution took place in England and the factory system and competitive conditions gradually asserted themselves in the majority of industrial markets. This is the second stage of capitalism, the stage that we call 'competitive', in the sense that, medieval privileges and institutional obstacles having been largely eliminated, the entry into different markets became relatively easy, productive units were relatively small and products were homogeneous. During this period several important changes took place: the most important was the development of a sector producing plant and machinery, which is what we now call the 'investment sector' – in the eighteenth century a limited number of units, hardly forming a sector, were producing 'machines' of the premodern type. When the investment sector became socially relevant, in England after the Napoleonic Wars, economic growth became a cyclical process, propelled mainly by that sector (compare Marx, 1977, 3, pp. 592–3). As appears from Schumpeter's monumental treatise on business cycles (1939), the growth of industrial economies emerged as a cyclical process in the sense that it was characterized, up to the First World War, by relatively regular fluctuations, lasting from seven to nine years – a striking regularity, considering the multitude of forces, economic and non-economic, impinging on the economy. After the First World War, beginning with 1929, the Great Depression took place, an economic earthquake that had its epicentre in the United States and was at the roots of extraordinary political events. Between the two world wars economic fluctuations became very irregular, also due to the increasing relevance of public interventions, and it is not easy to detect cycles. After the Second World War growth re-emerges as a cyclical process, but with new features and much less regularity as compared with the period preceding the First World War.

Since the investment sector is where machines are produced and since as a rule technological change is embodied in machines whose most recent models are also the most efficient ones, that sector became the principal source of technological change for the whole economy in the area of process innovations – different considerations apply to product innovations. Correspondingly, the machine makers were and still are the most important innovators in this area. At the same time, with the development of experimental science the inventions of professional scientists have become more and more frequent and their application to productive activities less and less rare.

During the competitive stage of capitalism, covering almost the whole of the nineteenth century, prices fluctuated, but their basic trend was decidedly downward until 1896 or 1897. Money and real wages also fluctuated: their trend was rising very slowly during the first half of the century, then rapidly. Labour productivity was increasing more than money wages, thus determining a decline in the cost of labour per unit of output and a decline in the trend of prices, in concordance with the views of Adam Smith.

Both the trend of wages and that of prices changed in what I call the stage of 'oligopolistic capitalism', starting towards the end of the nineteenth century and lasting, apparently, until the 1970s–1980s. This stage is characterized by an increasing concentration of firms and an increasing differentiation of products. In the stage of oligopolistic capitalism, apart from the abnormal period of the Great Depression, both money wages and prices were rising, the former more than the latter, the gap being attributable to the increase in labour productivity.

Whereas the process of concentration implies, in each sector, a decline in the number of firms, some of which became larger and larger, the process of differentiation has been accompanied by a systematic increase in the number of firms. But this did not necessarily imply increasing competition in the traditional sense. In fact, product differentiation and quality competition in many industries were partly replacing price competition, also due to the development of advertising made possible by the extraordinary expansion of the so-called 'mass media', like the modern newspaper, radio and, more recently, television, all created or strongly stimulated by major technological innovations.

The process of concentration itself is the effect of technological change and of what might be called 'dynamic economies of scale', since certain innovations necessarily imply an increase in the size of output. Such a process has been characterized by the reappearance, in new forms, of the joint-stock company, then – at the end of the nineteenth century, after a great merger movement – by trusts and cartels and, finally, by the giant multinational corporations. Among the propelling forces of this process we must include not only technological economies of scale, but also organizational, commercial and financial economies of scale.

Hand in hand with this process of concentration, a strengthening of trade unions has taken place, partly stimulated by that very process. In fact, trade unions are stronger in large firms, and they enjoy a certain market power over wages mainly as a result of market power over prices by firms. The whole process, which is at the roots of the changes in the trends of wages and prices (see chapter 3 below), was influenced, as regards the trade unions, also by political action and linked with the increasing influence of left-wing movements in the industrialized countries, particularly in Europe. The strengthening of the trade unions has caused an increasing downward rigidity and an increasing upward flexibility of money wages.

On average, especially after the Second World War, money wages were no longer relatively stationary as in the nineteenth century (real wages were increasing, owing to the fall in prices); as a rule, money wages today increase at a rate equal to and even higher than the increase in productivity. As a result, prices are either stationary (but only at the wholesale level) or increasing. In these new conditions a more or less intense structural inflationary pressure has appeared.

During the third stage of capitalism, then, the behaviour of prices and money wages is characteristically different from that of the previous stage; the trend of prices was no longer downward, but clearly upward. The only important exception was the sharp fall of prices in the Great Depression, but, as I will point out in chapter 3 (p. 76), the exception is explained by the different behaviour of the prices of raw materials and those of finished products – my previous considerations apply to the latter category.

During the stage of oligopolistic capitalism competition still works and can be vigorous, but it works in ways different from those of competitive capitalism. The main novelty is that in competitive capitalism firms are relatively small and produce homogeneous goods; in such conditions, firms cannot influence prices and workers cannot influence wages. Instead, in oligopolistic capitalism firms, to some extent, can influence prices and workers, mainly through trade unions, can influence wages. The fact is that the differentiation of needs and of jobs has been and is rapidly increasing owing to the increase of *per capita* income and the spread of product innovations.

In the third stage of the development of modern capitalism, and particularly after the Second World War, public expenditure and public intervention in research became more and more important for both military and civilian purposes. Public intervention in research also took the form of financial support of various kinds to the investment in laboratories of private firms and to universities. Let us remember that at least three of the most important inventions of our time – atomic energy, the numerically controlled machine tool and the laser – had their decisive breakthrough in two universities (Chicago, 1941, and the Massachusetts Institute of Technology, 1951 and 1965). The transistor, which is at the basis of the development of the electronic computer, was invented in 1951 in the laboratories of the Bell Corporation, a private corporation that, like the above-mentioned universities, had obtained relevant financial funds through contracts with the American government.

The contraposition between the state and the market, that is valid in several cases, is meaningless in the area of research, where we find cooperation even in those countries that more than others tend to favour market forces.

The revival of small firms: a new stage

The leading innovations of our time find their propelling centre in information technology (IT) and the computer industry. To be sure, the technological and economic changes that we are experiencing have become so profound and so rapid that they justify the hypothesis that we are entering a new stage, the fourth in my list. The best way to evaluate the importance of such changes is to look at the evolution in the structure of employment.

In highly industrialized countries employment in agriculture is reduced to a very small fraction of the total. Employment in industry is either stationary or declining, if only in relative terms, despite the fact that industry – and particularly manufacturing industry – remains the typical area of innovations which affect not only industry but the whole economy. Services, both private and public, have been expanding and employ the majority of the active population. As regards industry, a peculiar phenomenon is taking place in several countries – that is, a decrease in employment in large firms (with more than 1,000 employees) and an increase in employment in small firms, with total industrial employment declining or remaining more or less constant.

To explain these trends we have to recall the two types of division of labour described by Adam Smith. The first type – that is, the progressive specialization of productive operations among different firms – asserted itself during the Industrial Revolution and until, say, 1870; then for a long historical period – broadly speaking, from 1870 to 1970 – the former process was eclipsed by the second process, that leading to concentration, a process pushed by the division of labour occurring within firms, whose sizes increase. At present, however, the process of differentiation seems to have reappeared in new forms in many branches of industry, especially in those producing consumer goods. The new stage that Piore and Sabel (1984) defined as flexible specialization, and I (1981) called the stage of the revival of small firms, was opened up by certain innovations, such as microelectronics, which were largely the product of defence and space research. There are several economic reasons aiding such development:

- First, technological change is separating out many services formerly internal to industrial firms and therefore included, in both income and employment statistics, in the industrial sector; after the separation, such activities have been included among *services*. In this area we find certain segments of research activity, repair services and legal and technical services. Such a change, however, is not simply statistical or formal; it gives rise to an increasing number of highly specialized small firms which also become more and more important in terms of employment.

- Second, with increasing real incomes, an increasing number of consumers become interested not so much in price but in the *quality and design* of goods. This has provided new opportunities to small firms. In other words the differentiation of needs has been accompanied by that of goods, also due to innovations, and has given rise to a considerable market power both of firms and of workers, even independently of trade unions.

- Third, with rising real incomes, manual workers have shown an increasing resistance to accept repetitive and monotonous jobs, typically those required by the assembly line and other methods of mass production. As a consequence, industrialists have speeded up automation and, for certain operations, have introduced robots. But neither these decisions nor, in certain advanced countries, the immigration of workers from less developed countries has contained the increases in wages of repetitive jobs, while the import of the goods produced by the latter countries has increasd. All this, and especially the acceleration of automation, has helped to determine the decline in the employment of large firms. At the same time skilled workers are increasingly preferring to accept less repetitive and tedious jobs in *innovating small firms*.

- Finally, the *increasing pressure of trade unions*, which tends to be the more vigorous the larger the size of the firm, is a non-negligible factor for both the acceleration of automation and the decline in employment in large firms, and indirectly for the growth of small firms which, as we will see, has been powerfully favoured by the development of IT.

When small firms supply only or mainly a given large firm, they are satellites of such a firm; however, they become independent when they supply a variety of firms of different size and a number of individual consumers. On the other hand, small firms supplying large firms often obtain from such firms information or assistance to introduce technological innovations.

The new possibilities of growth opened up to small firms can have great importance for underdeveloped countries, whose markets, owing to low *per capita* incomes, are relatively limited: the fact that the relevance of the economies of scale is declining or that in several branches large size is no more a precondition for an efficient production is clearly an advantage for those countries.

In general, the revival of small firms does not imply that large firms lose their importance. As I said, their weight declines in terms of employment, not in terms of output, that in large firms continues to rise. A new merger movement has occurred and is now under way, with the emergence of giants of international relevance. In Europe, such a movement has been accelerated by the formation and the growth of the Common Market (see Sylos Labini, 1969 [1956], pp. 62–3) and is likely to receive a new impetus after the steps towards the unification of Europe, among which the creation of the Euro stands out. In certain industries the process of concentration, where static and dynamic scale economies have always been important, is giving rise to European and to world giants. In some of these industries, such as automobiles, scale economies have been enhanced by automation and robotization. Both the trend towards the diminution of employment in large firms and that towards the expansion of the size of those firms in terms of output or of activity, are particularly pronounced in the area of banks and other financial organizations.

In brief, we have two processes, only apparently contradictory: a new process of concentration and a new process of differentiation, the former pushing down, the latter pulling up, the level of employment. The algebraic sum tends to be positive especially owing to the service sector.

Schooling and research in the different stages of modern capitalism

During the first stage of modern capitalism, characterized by organizational and institutional changes in agriculture and by the growth of the early manufacturing activities, the relations between economic development and education were largely indirect. Major innovations were exceptional and were due to individual thinkers – 'philosophers' Smith calls them – minor innovations to common workmen. Illiteracy was the rule and only a minority of children were enrolled in elementary schools – Smith was advocating, not primarily for economic reasons, public intervention to generalize elementary education. Universities had few courses – law, philosophy, mathematics, natural sciences, medicine; universities in Italy were the best in Europe. In England universities to some extent still preserved their original purposes, i.e. of institutions for the education of churchmen.

During the stage of competitive capitalism, opened up, in England, by the Industrial Revolution, relations between scientific research and economic development were becoming less and less occasional. The triad considered by Joseph

Schumpeter – the inventor, the modern banker and the modern entrepreneur – assumed the main role in the process of economic development. Mechanical industry – the core of the investment sector – received a strong impulse in England by the orders of the Navy during the Napoleonic wars. Elementary education became available for the majority of the population and universities gave an increasing space to experimental science.

In the stage of oligopolistic capitalism, which began towards the end of the nineteenth century, entrepreneurs started new firms by exploiting major innovations – in the production of steel, in heavy mechanical industry, in chemistry, electricity and motor cars. In this stage, the elementary education of the whole adult population was completed – only tiny minorities remained illiterate. Pure research was developed in the universities and, in certain countries, also in private foundations and in the laboratories of large firms. Especially after the end of the Second World War and especially in the United States, military orders and contracts gave a great impulse to the growth of research, with an important fallout for civilian production.

In what I consider a new stage of modern capitalism, in which large firms continue to grow in terms of output but not in terms of employment and in which we observe a revival of small firms, public policy intended to promote research has been developed. In certain countries, such as the United States and some European countries, special organisms are created to promote the diffusion of innovations for the benefit of small firms that are unable to organize laboratories. (In the United States these 'business incubators' are created thanks to the cooperation of firms, local authorities and universities.)

If we consider the whole educational system in advanced countries after the Second World War, we notice that the number of university students grows rapidly everywhere and that certain universities strengthen their role in pure research, thus indirectly helping the development of applied research and of major innovations. At the same time, the role of the secondary and technical schools becomes essential for the speed of the diffusion of innovations. Here it is fitting to point out that the United Kingdom, that has some of the best universities in the world and an impressive number of Nobel prizes in experimental sciences, has not had a particularly brilliant performance as far as economic development is concerned: on the whole, after the Second World War, the increase of productivity has been either equal to or, more often, below the increase observable in several other European countries, in the United States and in Japan. In England the production of inventions and of innovations is good; less good is the process of diffusion of innovations. I think that this can be explained if we consider the record in the area of secondary and technical schools; this UK record is not particularly favourable, as appears from the data of table 31 of the 1998 UN *Human Development Report*.

The process of diffusion of innovations in a given country is, then, to be distinguished from the process of their production; this in its turn depends on the creation of inventions, that today as a rule takes place in public and private laboratories. However, a country can adopt the policy of imitating the innovations carried out by others – this was the policy adopted by Japan after the Second World War. But imitation necessarily implies adaptations and thus elements of innovation; when such elements become prevalent, we can speak of production of innovation rather than of imitation.

From the standpoint of both economic growth and civic development of a given country, the production of innovations is by far more important than the consumption of goods produced by innovating industries: it is not the availability that matters, but the productive capacity, which can grow in the course of time. From the standpoint of economic growth the production of innovations is important especially because it can offer, in international competition, a shelter or a weapon much more efficient than that given by the consumption of new goods produced by other countries, even if these are investment goods. From the civic standpoint we have to consider that the production of innovations necessarily implies research activities that have widespread cultural fallouts and improvement in the quality of labour – I refer not only to the growth of research workers, but also to that of technicians and of highly skilled workers.

Technological innovations and institutional innovations

In the production and in the diffusion of innovations research and schooling have the key role. For good and bad, innovations represent the essence of modern civilization and, particularly, of economic development. We have to distinguish between technological and institutional innovations. By referring to 'epoch-making innovations' Schumpeter was considering three industrial revolutions. The first, the English Industrial Revolution, took place, in a purely indicative way, between 1770 and 1830 and received its main impulse from the steam engine applied to the textile industry and to the first mechanical industry. The second revolution, that occurred between 1830 and the end of the nineteenth century, was pushed by the application of the steam engine to the means of transportation on land (railways) and by sea (steamships). The third revolution – 1900–50 – was pushed by chemistry, electricity and the internal combustion engine, applied to automobiles and aeroplanes. We may add a fourth revolution, in which we live, pushed by new types of aeroplanes and, above all, by IT. It is fitting to emphasize that this extraordinary and multi-form innovation gives rise to remarkable savings in the time of production and of delivery, makes accessible to small firms the advantages of economies of scale previously restricted to large firms, modifies already existing goods and services and generates new goods and services in a continual stream, with consequences that concern and sometime disturb the life of persons no less than economic activities.

These great technological innovations have been accompanied and, so to say, supported by institutional innovations, that are embodied in law. Here I will recall three such innovations: modern banking – the rise of the bank that creates money in the sense that it transforms the debts of firms into deposits that can be used as a means of payment – the stock exchange and the modern joint-stock company.

The bank that creates money asserted itself already in the first stage of modern capitalism and subsequently expanded rapidly, radically changing its features. The second innovation, the stock exchange, emerged towards the end of the seventeenth century, but had a strong expansion only in the second half of the nineteenth century, with the development of steamships and of railways, that required firms of large size. Hand in hand with the stock exchange the modern joint-stock company appeared and developed. At the origin of both innovations – stock exchange and joint-stock company – are activities that are in need of large and increasing financial means and therefore require rapid investment and disinvestment decisions.

Such developments have been accelerated and amplified by large mergers and then by the growth of multi-national companies. Such developments recently have been integrated by the appearance of new financial intermediaries.

Changes in institutions condition and are conditioned by the overall development of the economy, although the development of particular industries, such as railways, have played a special role in promoting certain institutional changes. In the case of certain industries that are important not only from the point of view of their size, but also because of the consequences that they can have on the whole of social life – such as electricity – the development of such industries is bound to be regulated by laws that occasionally have to be modified. I tried some years ago to sketch the development of the British electrical industry through the laws that have accompanied it, sometimes by favouring it, at other times by restraining it (Sylos Labini, 1974).

The most important institutional changes, however, refer, not to a particular industry or a particular sector, but to the whole economy. It is a process of continuous change, that has to be seen in the framework of the whole cultural evolution, of which the institutional changes are only one aspect.

2

Culture, institutions and resources

The cultural background: the cases of the United States and Costa Rica

Cultural development is the origin of economic development – this is the leitmotiv of this book. 'Culture', however, if conceived in a broad sense, is a vague and elusive concept and vagueness is the enemy of serious scholarship. I will therefore start by considering particular instances of the relations between culture, institutions and economic growth.

In his long discussion of the problems of agricultural development, which is the basis of the economic growth of every society, Adam Smith illustrated the role of the legal institutions regulating transfers of property rights on lands via the market or heredity; at the same time he posed the question of the types of contracts most suitable to favour agricultural development. The basic idea is that such development is promoted mainly by small owners. All regulations and fetters of feudal origin, which keep large areas of land outside the market and forbid the expansion of small owners, represent obstacles to agricultural development.

As for the relations between landowners and tenants, Smith considered a variety of contracts. The most unfavourable to growth were in his opinion those contracts affording tenants no guarantee of duration, such as those of 'tenants-at-will', so that cultivators had no interest in introducing improvements. At the other extreme were 'long leases', in which cultivators, and their heirs, were entitled to enjoy the fruits of the improvements that they were introducing. Among the holders of long leases, Smith mentioned the yeomen, who had rights similar to those of landowners, were serving in the army as horse knights and were entitled to vote for the parliament. Smith goes so far as to state that 'those laws and customs so favourable to the yeomanry have perhaps contributed to the present grandeur of England more than all their boasted regulations of commerce taken together' (1961 [1776], book III, ch. II).

As for transfers of property rights of land via heredity, the most disadvantageous form from the point of view of development was, for Smith, the right of primogeniture, which hindered the growth of small owners. This effect was consolidated by the constraint of inalienability ('entail'), that was applied even after land was transmitted by heredity. Originally those two institutions were justified by reasons of security, in the sense that large estates were guaranteeing to the owners, in the Middle Ages when local wars were the rule, a certain security not obtainable in other ways. However, Smith maintained that, with the gradual strengthening of the social order in several parts of Europe, that justification had disappeared; thus, if those institutions were surviving, this was due not only to forces of inertia but also to reasons of pride of a number of aristocratic families. In any case, an institutional reform can be successful only if it inserts itself in an evolution already under way.

For Smith, then, the property right of land was not important in itself, but in the different forms that it assumed and in the different contracts based on that right. Paradoxically, even the absence of private property of land – an impossible thing in the countries where the rule of '*nulle terre sans seigneur*' was in force – can favour agricultural development, if the duration of the possession of land is in some way guaranteed. This was the case of free lands in those that Smith called 'our American colonies'.

In this light it is worthwhile to reconsider briefly the analysis worked out by Smith to explain the 'causes of the prosperity of the new colonies' (1961 [1776], book IV, ch. VIII, part II) with the help of a few quotations by Smith and by Alexis de Tocqueville (Tocqueville, 1951), which complement each other perfectly.

(1)   'The English puritans, restrained at home, fled for freedom to America and established there the four governments of New England' [they fled for freedom, we may add, and not to escape hunger or misery or, as adventurers, rapidly to enrich themselves] (Smith, 1961 [1776], book IV, ch. VII, part II, p. 102).

(2)   'The colonies owe to the policy of Europe the education and the great views of their active and enterprising founders' (Smith, 1961 [1776], book IV, ch. VII, part II, p. 103).

(3)   'Almost all colonies have had as their early inhabitants men with no education and no resources, that were pushed by misery or misconduct out of their native countries, or else greedy speculators and adventurers' (Tocqueville, 1951, p. 44).

(4)   'The emigrants who settled down on the shores of New England all belonged . . . to the relatively well-to-do classes of their mother country. Their meeting in the American land presented straight from the beginning the singular phenomenon of a society without very wealthy men and without lower classes, with no poor and no rich people' (Tocqueville, 1951, p. 45).

Tocqueville himself emphasized that this was not the case for Virginia and other southern regions of the United States. In such regions, colonists were adventurers who tried to enrich themselves mainly by searching for mines of precious metals or by organizing plantations of tropical crops using imported negro slaves as a labour force. For a long period the growth of southern regions was much slower than that of the northern regions, where the original immigrants were persons of a much higher cultural level. It is well to point out that such a dualism can in no way be attributed to racial differences, since the colonists were Anglo-Saxon in both the North and in the South.

(5)   'The colonists [in the northern regions] carry with them a knowledge of agriculture and of other useful arts, . . . some notions of the regular government . . ., of the system of law which supports it, and of a regular administration of justice' (Smith, 1961 [1776], book IV, ch. VII, part II, p. 76).

(6)   'In the American colonies land is plentiful and free — the cost of a piece of land consists almost exclusively in the operations necessary for making it suitable for cultivation. [As a result,] every colonist gets more land than he can possibly cultivate . . . He is eager, therefore, to collect labourers from all quarters and to reward them with the most liberal wages. But those most liberal wages, joined with the plenty and cheapness of land, soon make those labourers leave him to become landlords themselves, and to reward, with equal liberality, other labourers' (Smith, 1961 [1776], book IV, ch. VII, part II, pp. 76–7).

The availability of free land and the consequent difficulty of keeping dependent workers for long lie also at the foundation of Marx's theory of colonization; Marx, however, reached conclusions that experience has shown to be untenable, as I showed in my earlier book on underdevelopment (Sylos Labini, 1983a, ch. III).

For these reasons, Smith maintained that, to keep labourers as dependent workers at least for a period, landlords had 'to treat the inferior with . . . generosity and humanity' and 'to pay not only high also increasing wages'. This occurred inside and outside agriculture, since wages tend to move together in all branches of the economy. Thus a 'virtuous circle' emerged in which rising wages stimulated productivity increases and such increases enabled masters to pay rising wages. At the beginning such a process was put into motion by the availability of free land. In the American colonies wages were then rising since the start of modern capitalism, whereas in Europe wages were quasi-stationary, owing to the great number of persons ready to be employed in the new capitalist firms; these persons were expelled by an agriculture that was undergoing a deep transformation from a quasi-feudal towards a capitalist set-up. The very relations between masters and dependent workers in America were originally shaped in a way that we do not find in Europe, where class divisions were still pronounced, as a relic of feudal times. In the American colonies, which subsequently became the United States of America, class divisions have always been very weak and the Marxian class struggle of limited relevance: the fact is that from the beginning masters were compelled, so to say, to treat dependent workers 'with generosity and humanity'.

During the second part of the nineteenth century in the United States free land practically disappeared. However, once put into motion, the process of productivity enhancement went on, stimulated by a number of other factors, already in operation in the preliminary stage of modern capitalism and then becoming more and more important, among which we have to include the increase in income.

To be sure, owing to the gradual disappearance of free land and the large influx of poor European immigrants wages, and especially wages of common workers, increased more slowly during the last two decades of the nineteenth century and the first decade of the twentieth century than in the previous period, and productivity growth lost this stimulus. As for the availability of free land, an economist, Rothbarth, and an economic historian, Habbakuk, have pointed out that the availability of land did have an important role in explaining the different behaviour of productivity in Great Britain and in the

United States; but they have emphasized the physical rather than the institutional availability, which is instead precisely what matters; on the other hand, these two scholars do not mention the role of the culture of the English emigrants who settled down in the northern regions of America (Rothbarth, 1946, p. 385; Habbakuk, 1967, pp. 7–8).

In the Spanish and Portuguese colonies of America the 'virtuous circle' described above was hampered not by physical scarcity of good land – indeed, the quantity of good land was even greater than that of the English colonies of North America – but by institutional limitations in a broad sense, including such legal and fiscal rules as the possibility of engrossing uncultivated land, the right of primogeniture and heavy taxation. These institutional limitations rendered land artificially scarce and expensive in South and Central America. As a result, wages of dependent workers could remain at low levels for a relatively long time, a situation aggravated by the fact that in the large estates of the '*conquistadores*' slaves and feudal serfs were allowed. At that time slaves were also allowed in the southern regions of the United States, where colonists, as I have already observed, were people of inferior culture compared with those of the northern regions.

Today situations not much different from that just described are found in Asia and Africa, that is, in the former tropical colonies of several European countries. In these colonies a kind of capitalistic sector was formed to produce agricultural and mineral raw materials, while a traditional (subsistence) sector continued to exist, organized in primitive communities. The traditional sector, essentially for lack of 'knowledge of agriculture and other useful arts' (Smith, 1961 [1776]), was incapable of making improvement in production, and productivity remained stagnant. In the capitalist sector wages were somewhat higher than the incomes prevailing in the traditional one, so that some labour could be lured into moving into the capitalist sector (Lewis, 1954). But these wages could be moderately higher than the incomes in the traditional sector and could remain relatively stable in the face of an expansion in the capitalist sector only as long as the potential labourers in the traditional sector were numerous enough and, if necessary, as long as they could be supplemented by small tradesmen and pedlars from the towns and by increases of population.

Going back to Latin America, we have to recall that institutions of a feudal type were imported from Spain and Portugal to serve the interest of the dominant classes, that is, to enable them better to control and organize the natives who did not belong to the seignorial properties. I refer, for instance, to *ejido*, an institution founded on the common use of land (similar to the old 'commons' in Great Britain, though in the Middle Ages every European country had an institution of that kind). In Mexico *ejido* was utilized as one of the main instruments for carrying out several agrarian reforms in the twentieth century: in this aspect, too, past is present.

But there is more. In the colonial period the administrative system was highly centralized: even local offices were under strict control of the central administrations, in their turn controlled by the central European governments through powers entrusted to big landowners or to public servants responsible to big landowners. Some such centralization remains even today, in spite of all the transformations that have occurred over the course of centuries. It should be noted, too, that in Spain the emigration towards her colonies was not free but selected by a central organ of control which systematically excluded non-conformist people. All this had, and still has, a significant influence on the social make-up in Latin American countries.

The institutional impediments to mobility and to the subdivision of land blocked the growth of small agricultural owners, that in other countries often promoted activities of an industrial type by themselves or their children. This stimulated a pathological growth of bureaucrats and small tradesmen.

A study of the historical roots of Latino-american countries, then, can contribute to explaining both the lag in and the slowness of their growth process and the fragility of their democratic institutions – a fragility made more serious after the Second World War by the formation of relatively small numbers of Marxist intellectuals, almost always belonging to the middle classes, that were preaching the necessity of fighting US predominance ('imperialism') by having recourse to terrorism, thus scaring to death large strata of the middle classes and, in this way, opening the doors to autocratic dictatorships. The knapsack of history that we carry on our shoulders is much heavier than we are ready to admit.

However, we can also find a kind of exception within Latin America: Costa Rica. In my view, this country has had in common with the United States the fact that in its early colonial times large estates did not appear. The serious inequality in land distribution and the very limited growth of smallholdings that are at the origin of the conflictual economic evolution of many Latin American countries was avoided in Costa Rica, since the initial development of the country was carried out by relatively small landowners. *Conquistadores* were not attracted by a land that, in spite of the name subsequently adopted, was not really 'rich', either in mines or in fertility – mountains and hills are the dominant topography and even now cultivated land represents only a fraction of the total. Moreover, in a land of this type *indios* to exploit as slaves or as serfs were few. Small owners settled after the initial stage of colonization, when coffee, which can be cultivated in the hills, proved to be profitable. The fact that it was not particularly rich probably explains why Costa Rica escaped the invasions and avoided the problems that large flows of immigrants could have created. The lack of large estates and the growth of smallholdings favoured democratic forms of government and a relatively low intensity of social conflict. In general, Costa Rica presents many indicators of human development decidedly better than those that the degree of economic development reached would normally allow. Yet, such a degree is not high: Costa Rica does not yet belong to the club of advanced countries. Why? This question is complex and difficult. My answer will come shortly.

The relationships between economic, human and civic development: favourable and unfavourable 'deviations'

Adam Smith used *per capita* income as an index indicator of economic development. In '*per capita* income' he included material commodities, but not services. Considering the great conceptual and statistical difficulties in the measurement of services, difficulties that in many respects are related to the reasons that induced Smith to exclude services from income, it would be advisable to analyse separately the behaviour of the two flows – commodities and services. As economic development goes on, the weight of services, measured in terms of employment, increases and therefore the meaning of '*per capita* income' becomes more and more ambiguous. However, in international comparisons *per capita* incomes measured in terms of purchasing power parities (PPPs) reduce the ambiguity, owing to the method with which they include services as well as goods that cannot enter into international trade (see the techical notes in the appendix of the World Bank's *World Development Report*, 1998).

It is fitting to point out that Smith was well aware that a relatively high *per capita* income was no more than a prerequisite of what I would call 'civic development', which is much more important than economic development and is a broader concept, since it includes not only wealth, health, education but also cultural and political freedom.[1]

This means that we cannot expect to find a strict relation between *per capita* income and those non-economic aspects of civic development that can be quantified. If we draw diagrams where we relate *per capita* income to non-economic phenomena of different countries, we notice that the points do not lie on straight lines but, rather, cluster in areas delimited by two curves, sloping downward or upward. This means that non-economic phenomena are influenced but not really determined by *per capita* income. More than that: some of the points lie clearly off the line and represent true 'deviations', that can be seen as a consequence of very particular economic factors – or, more often, of cultural and institutional factors. Such reflections can help us to get rid of the conviction, held not only by Marxists, but also by several non-Marxist scholars, of the prevalent role of the so-called 'economic factor' in explaining social phenomena. It is high time that we recognized the relevance of purely political forces that strictly speaking are to be related to cultural traditions – and, for good or ill, also to the particular personalities of leaders and of influential intellectuals.

In diagrams such as these, one for each of the non-economic phenomena that I intend to examine (see figures 2.1–2.4, pp. 45–6), the abscissa shows an index number of *per capita* income, where 100 is that of the United States and PPPs are taken as conversion factors instead of official exchange rates – the differences being mostly imputable to cross-country valuation of services and non-tradable goods and services. The ordinates show the non-economic phenomena that we intend to study: life expectancy, infant mor-

[1] As Alessandro Roncaglia pointed out, Smith writes in his *Lectures on Rethoric and Belles Lettres* (1983, p. 137): 'Opulence and commerce commonly precede the improvement of art and refinement of every sort. I do not mean that the improvement of arts and refinements of manners are the necessary consequence of commerce . . ., only that it is a necessary requisite.'

tality, fertility rate and adult female illiteracy. In each diagram, two lines are drawn, each starting from the maximum (or the minimum) of the phenomenon examined. The lines are drawn in such a way as to leave out a small number of 'deviations' indicating countries that, given their *per capita* incomes, show either an abnormally good, or an abnormally bad, performance. The next step is to understand the reasons for the deviations.

Before discussing this matter, we need to consider an analysis by Giorgio Fuà, who found that an increase in *per capita* income was accompanied by an increase in life expectancy, but only up to a certain level – today 30–40 per cent of US *per capita* income, all incomes measured in PPPs (see Fuà, 1993). Beyond this level, even if *per capita* income increases life expectancy does not increase. The ceiling today is about 78 years; in the course of time it has tended to shift upwards for all countries: it was 60 years in the 1930s and 70 years in the 1950s. The ceiling depends on the world patrimony of medical knowledge and its upward shifts depend on research conducted mainly by the most developed countries. The actual levels of life expectancy reached by the different countries depend on the actual utilization of that knowledge – that is, its growth, up to the given ceiling, depends on economic conditions.

Let us discuss, then, the question of deviations, beginning with those concerning life expectancy. Clearly, the higher *per capita* income, the greater the utilization of medical knowledge – in terms of medicines and well equipped hospitals – the higher the life expectancy. However, medical knowledge is not everything: availability of food, decent housing, safe water as well as the possibility of following a hygienic lifestyle, including exercise and sport, are also important; and all these items depend on economic conditions.

In figure 2.1 the two curves express the boundaries of the relations between *per capita* income, as a percentage of that of the United States, and life expectancy. When *per capita* income exceeds 40 per cent of that of the United States the upper curve approaches a straight line, the 'ceiling' discussed above. No deviations can be observed above this portion of the upper curve, but some deviations can be found below the lower curve.

In the area of the favourable deviations we find Sri Lanka and Costa Rica. Among the unfavourable deviations there are Namibia, Gabon and the United Arab Emirates. The main reason is that these countries produce high-value goods – diamonds in Namibia, oil in the other countries – that swell *per capita* income beyond the welfare of the population: as a rule, production in each of these countries is controlled by a very few people, so that income distribution is very unequal and income *per capita* of the majority of the population is very low. As for South Africa, which also appears as an unfavourable deviation, we have to take into account the fact that the living conditions of the blacks, who represent the majority of the population, are bad and their life expectancy affects the average.

In a similar analysis that I conducted some years ago using 1990 data (Sylos Labini, 1993a), some of the oil-producing countries, such as Saudi Arabia, Iran and Libya, emerged as unfavourable deviations since life expectancy was lower – though not much lower – than what was to be expected on the basis of *per capita* income. Today these countries are no longer among the unfavourable deviations, owing probably to two factors. First, their relatively high *per capita* income was caused by high oil prices; in the mid- and late 1990s the price of oil went down, while the reference income, that of the United States, increased – in general more than that of the oil-producing countries, so that their relative positions in the international classifications fell (at present – autumn 1999 – oil prices are again on the rise). Second, thanks also to the financial boost afforded by oil to public revenue, the government of those countries continued to invest in health facilities, with the consequence that life expectancy, already

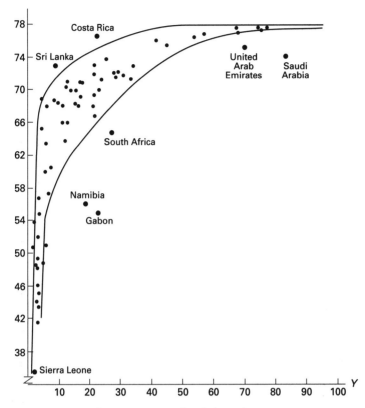

Figure 2.1 Life expectancy at birth (years)
Note: Y is *per capita* income, 1997, per cent of US *per capita* income, PPP dollars.
Source: World Development Report, 1995–7.

rising, rose even more in recent years. These reflections show that the performance of various phenomena of the different countries, classified according to their degree of economic growth, may open the door to fruitful analyses going far beyond those that can be inferred simply by comparing the *per capita* income of different countries.

The second phenomenon that I examined is infant mortality (figure 2.2). Here, Sri Lanka and Costa Rica are on the

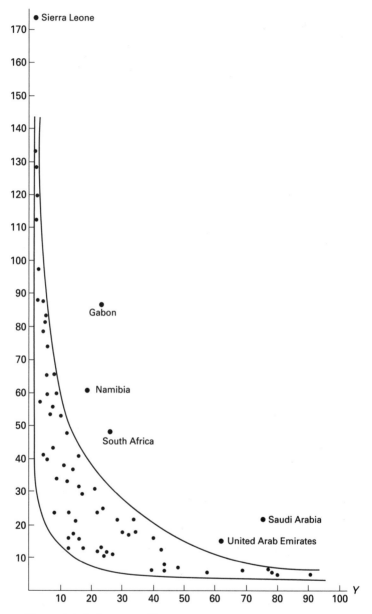

Figure 2.2 Infant mortality
Source: World Development Report, 1995–7.

border of the minimum line, whereas located above the maximum line – i.e. as negative deviations – we find, as in the case of life expectancy and for similar reasons, Gabon, South Africa, Namibia, the United Arab Emirates and Saudi Arabia.

The third phenomenon examined is the fertility rate (figure 2.3). As the pressure of population in underdeveloped countries does not favour economic development – or, more generally, civic development – but constitutes a very serious impediment to it, since it generates an increasing mass of poor people, we gauge positively the declines that occur in fertility and birth rates. The trouble is that in many countries these rates are still rising, in some they are stable and in several others they are declining, but very slowly, so that their population continues to grow, though at a falling rate. In all cases, measures to determine, or to hasten, the decline of the two rates are to be recommended. We will see that, to this effect, the degree of education of women can play an important role. This is why it is worthwhile to examine also the relationship between *per capita* income and female illiteracy, the last of the four phenomena of our study (figure 2.4).

In underdeveloped countries adult illiteracy is high among both sexes, but in several countries illiteracy is significantly higher in the female population – the ratio is as high as 1.5 : 1 or even 2 : 1; in certain countries female illiteracy reaches or even surpasses 90 per cent. The reasons for this divergence are always cultural; in particular, they are to be related either to traditions that go back to the dawn of time, or to the political teaching of certain religions. The state of inferiority in which women are kept in many societies in one way or another, often even institutionally, is not relevant only for reasons of justice, but for economic reasons, given the excessive demographic pressure that it generates and the limited contribution that in those conditions women can make to economic growth.

As with fertility rates, favourable deviations include Costa Rica, Sri Lanka, China (on the border line) and a group of

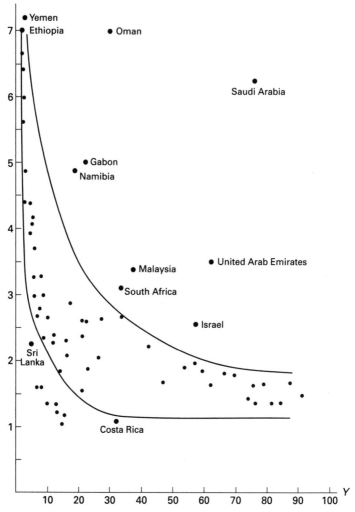

Figure 2.3 Fertility rate (birth per woman)
Source: World Development Report, 1995–7.

countries that were in the sphere of influence of the former Soviet Union; the unfavourable deviations include Mozambique, Uganda, Yemen and Ethiopia. In the case of adult female illiteracy, among the favourable deviations we

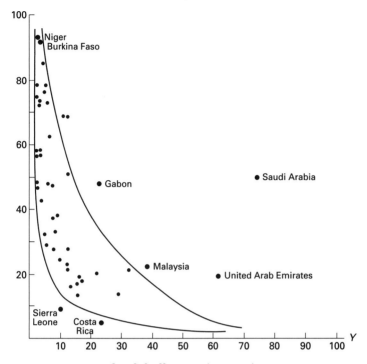

Figure 2.4 Female adult illiteracy (per cent)
Source: World Development Report, 1995–7.

find Costa Rica, Sri Lanka and China; among the unfavourable deviations, Niger (93 per cent), Burkina Faso (91), Sierra Leone (90) and Nepal (86) (when the points of the countries considered are very near to the upper or to the lower curve, they are not indicated in the diagrams).

It is fitting to point out that the favourable deviations observable in the left-hand corner of figure 2.3 (fertility rates), below the lower curve refer, apart from Sri Lanka, to countries of the former Soviet bloc. Probably the explanation could be found in the demographic policy followed by the communist governments and in the fact that most of these countries suffered an economic setback after the dissolution of the Soviet bloc.

In this review of the relations that exist between *per capita* income and some of the most important indicators of civic development, we find two countries that emerge systematically as favourable deviations from the norm – Costa Rica and Sri Lanka.

Costa Rica represents a deviation not only in terms of the indicators examined, but also in other important respects, especially if compared with its neighbours such as Nicaragua and Guatemala. Costa Rica has experienced a stable democratic evolution; repressions and civil wars, frequent in the other two countries, have been absent in Costa Rica, where the army (as a rule a reactionary force in Latin America, employed more for internal political purposes than for external wars) was abolished in 1948. The contrast with the evolution of Nicaragua and Guatemala could not be sharper. In all these countries, the political and cultural establishment is composed of people of Spanish origin. Again, as in the case of the Northern and Southern regions of the United States, racial differences cannot be the explanation either.

In my view, a main reason why we find Costa Rica among the positive deviations lies in the original institutional arrangement concerning land. Yet, if Costa Rica is still relatively underdeveloped from the economic standpoint, the reason, I believe, is education, especially higher education. If, in a similar way to what occurred in the United States, the original land distribution in Costa Rica was favourable to economic growth and to democracy, the conditions concerning culture that were present in the initial stage of the development of the United States were lacking in Costa Rica, since the colonists that settled there had a very low degree of education. Thus the country did not have the advantage that the United States, and particularly New England, had, a relatively good level of education of the early colonists. Naturally, in the course of time Costa Rica has remedied this deficiency. Today elementary and intermediate education do not appear to be particularly weak, but I believe that it is worthwhile to make the strongest effort to strengthen and to develop the institutions for higher education and for research.

As for Sri Lanka, the other country showing several favourable deviations on the social development indicators, we have to consider its relatively egalitarian traditions that are related, in my judgement, first to the prevailing Buddhist religion, which has essentially democratic and even liberal (tolerant) characteristics, in contrast to the Hinduism prevailing in India, for example, which attributes a relevant role to castes. In Sri Lanka, traditions of tolerance were reinforced in social life in the past by certain kings, and in more recent times by certain left-wing governments. Other countries, too, where Buddhism has had a socially pervasive influence, such as Thailand and Myanmar (formerly Burma) have relatively favourable indicators; for somewhat different reasons this applies also to Kerala, one of the Indian states, that shows social indicators much better than those of the others (Kannan, 1995). Japan also benefited from a strong Buddhist influence. The same indicators also illustrate the negative consequences of religions characterized by intolerance, among them Hinduism and Islamism in their most integralistic varieties. One of the indicators of civic backwardness is the social position of women in comparison with that of men; the inferiority of women is, at the same time, one of the consequences and one of the causes of civic backwardness. (Among the obstacles that certain religions put in the way of the growth process we find, apart from the state of inferiority of women, the prohibition of the rate of interest, based on a sophism similar to that originally proposed by Aristotle, see p. 56).

An inspection of figures 2.1–2.4 shows that a ceiling similar to that suggested by Fuà in the case of life expectancy can probably be applied to several other phenomena. This concept, as well as the question of deviations, emphasizes that economic growth is really important from the standpoint of human development up to a certain critical level: beyond that level, it is less and less important. However, the terrible problem of poverty of a share of the population is not automatically solved by sustained growth. Thus, before that critical level is reached, efforts by national and international, private and public decision centres should concern both growth and the share of poverty; after that level, those efforts should be concentrated on the latter alone.

Race and the different evolution of different societies.

Today we observe a growing number of Asian and Latin American countries showing an increasing dynamism in their development. Economic stagnation is to be found mostly in Sub-Saharan Africa; in some parts of the region *per capita* income is even declining. Why is this so? More generally: why is there such a great variety in economic and civic developments in the different countries of the world?

The present writer does not believe in racial explanations. Superiority or inferiority of different populations cannot be gauged using a unique criterion. Thus, from the physical point of view, Africans are by no means inferior, often they are superior to white people: it is enough to look to athletic competitions and to the list of world champions – a considerable number of them are Blacks.

There are two cultures, it has been said, the humanistic and the scientific culture; if we admit that social sciences can be viewed as autonomous, the types of culture become three. Humanistic culture includes literature, poetry, music, painting and other arts; scientific culture is founded on experiments and presupposes laboratories, special instruments and various supporting structures that require significant economic development; it presupposes a special kind of division of labour, close relations as well as inter-personal competition among researchers, who have to go through a long period of study, university selection and be able to adapt to rigorous discipline in complex organizations, where knowledge is transmitted and enlarged. Thus research comes out of a process of evolution in which both ideas and institutions on one side and economic growth on the other are combined. The progress in experimental science is to be seen principally as a social phenomenon. In humanistic disciplines, on the contrary, talented individuals play the main role. For certain aspects of social sciences, the features of experimental science seem to prevail. People of underdeveloped countries can excel in humanistic culture no less than those of advanced countries, but today they find it very difficult to excel in experimental science, the science that originates new technologies. It should be noted, however, that in underdeveloped countries it is less rare to find excellent scholars in social than in physical sciences.

All things considered, we cannot escape the conclusion that a fundamental handicap of Africans and of several other populations in our historical period may lie in an inferior scientific culture, which negatively conditions economic growth, by limiting the capacity to innovate. The scientific and technological superiority that was developed in the past by the Europeans of Europe and those transplanted in North America and maintained over time has *de facto* 'subjugated' other populations: that was the source of the force which Adam Smith spoke of.

It is culture in this particular sense that counts. The previous question, then, can be transformed into the following one: why was Europe able to enter into the spiral of scientific progress, especially vigorous in the last 500 years (and, if we consider the systematic application of many scientific discoveries to economic activity, in the last 200 years), with the proviso that the applications to economic activity have often given rise to a positive feedback on scientific progress itself?

Why, then, in Europe first? And why were an increasing number of countries able to imitate that process, often creatively, as in the case of Japan, whereas up to now in other countries this process of imitation has been very slow – with some of them remaining stagnant or even going backwards in terms of *per capita* income? I do not feel confident enough to try to answer such questions, but I feel sure that the answer is to be found in the field of culture and of cultural evolution: race is not part of the answer. That the concept of race has no scientific basis has been demonstrated by biologists. My thesis is that the analysis of the evolution of various societies brings a similar conclusion from the standpoint of social sciences. The conclusion is even stronger, since the differences observable among populations, that induce some people into believing that they are due to race, are precisely those originated by different cultural evolutions.

As for Africa, and especially for the Sub-Saharan region, we have to emphasize that in several countries the ancient tribal system is still in place and, with it, the struggle between different ethnic groups. The situation has been aggravated, in our time, by the artificial boundaries created by European powers when they conquered certain territories: the boundaries of the colonies subsequently became the boundaries of many contemporary African countries, compelling different ethnic groups and tribes to live together. Ethnic conflicts are often the result of a struggle for political supremacy of one group over another. Conflicts between different social classes are very rare and the Marxian class struggle practically does not exist in Africa. In these countries dependent workers are, as a rule, small minorities (no more than 10 or 20 per cent) and the conflicts between them and the 'capitalists' are hardly relevant from the social point of view. Ethnic conflicts, on the contrary, are important and sometimes dramatic: they create serious obstacles to cultural and scientific development, even of an imitative type, and even to economic growth. Ethnic conflicts characterize the social life of a number of advanced countries as well; but in such countries their impact on growth is much more limited.

Altogether, if we take a world perspective, ethnic conflicts are far more important than class struggle and the conflicts over the distribution of income that arise in developing countries. The fact that often – though not always – ethnic conflicts appear to be religious conflicts does not change the substance of the problem. Economic factors do enter into the picture, but often only collaterally. In certain cases foreign powers or internal groups stir up ethnic conflict to obtain economic advantage.

The role of particular ethnic groups in the process of development

In certain countries the evolution of particular ethnic groups must be examined in combination with the evolution of specific economic activities. Thus, in a number of Asian and African countries both wholesale and retail trade has been, and remains, in the hands of foreign ethnic groups: Chinese in Indonesia and in several other South Eastern Asian countries, Indians in South Africa, Mozambique, Uganda and Kenya, Armenians in different areas of the Middle East and of Europe, Arabians in several Sub-Saharan countries, Jews in many European and in American countries.

During the evolution that most economies have undergone in the course of centuries, the need to develop long-distance traffic has emerged regularly, if at different points of the process. When sea traffic was not possible and the growth traffic required land transportation and some sort of commercial organization, alien groups proved to be the most suitable to perform those functions. In the prevailing rural stationary economies the most suitable persons to meet such needs were precisely individuals without local roots, coming from other countries. Several members of these groups who, being aliens and often of a different religion, were precluded from the ownership of land and from practising several professions and public functions, were able to become relatively rich through commercial traffic; sometimes they added banking to their mercantile activity.

In fact, for centuries in Europe Jews were free to lend money for interest, while Christians in principle were not allowed to do so owing to the prohibition of the Church, that accepted Aristotle's dictum '*pecunia non parit pecuniam*'. This sophism – accepted also by other religions – is logically untenable, but historically understandable in prevailingly agricultural economies in which loans were as a rule made to consumers, almost always very poor, whereas today the majority of loans are made to firms – in the former case, interest is paid out of incomes independent of loans, in the latter, out of profits, arising from an activity financed by loans. In those conditions traders were often able to gain both from commerce and from money lending, since in the countryside they enjoyed a sort of monopsonistic power and were in a position to exploit the peasants by buying their products at very low prices; at the same time peasants were often indebted to them and had to pay high interest rates. They were thus regarded with hostility by the local population, mostly peasants, an hostility aggravated by the fact that they were foreigners and often with a skin of different colour. The dominant local groups tended to exploit those alien groups economically and financially and, in times of dramatic social tensions, to use them as scapegoats: this was the origin of pogroms against Jews in Europe and Chinese in Malaysia and Indonesia. In Indonesia there was a massacre of half a million Chinese in 1965, and local violence against the Chinese community in 1998. (In 1965 the Chinese were branded as 'communist', since the idea was, and perhaps still is, that a Chinese outside the mother country was supposed to be loyal to China whatever his or her ideology; Mao was the ruler at that time and the internal political struggles in Indonesia were conditioned by international rivalries.)

In Europe the hostility of the masses towards the Jews became deeply rooted: here the religious hostility of the Christians played a particularly important role since the Hebraic religion was considered to be opposed to Christianity, in spite of the fact that Christ was a Jew. Especially in the last 200 years, in addition to the hostility of the masses of poor peasants a new type of hostility surfaced – that of non-negligible sections of the cultivated middle classes. This hostility was fed by the acute competition of the Jews in certain intellectual and professional activities where they excelled. Their religion, founded much more than in other ethnic groups on study, since childhood, as a way to interpret the sacred texts, probably helped to develop certain intellectual powers. In turn, Jewish religion as well as Jewish culture – here much more than in other cases, the two aspects overlap – became a sort of cement uniting the Jewish groups and helping them to resist the hostility of the non-Jewish population. The great care that Jews have devoted to education and to cultural activities in general have undoubtedly contributed to raising their average intellectual level in the long run.

Under the double pressure of hostility from both the higher classes and the poorest strata of the population, the process of selection – which tends to promote not the strongest in muscles but the most vigorous in brains – was particularly severe for all alien groups, with the consequence that the average level of intelligence, however measured, rose considerably. These observations apply to many, if not most alien groups, but certainly the Jews and the Chinese represent the most important and best known cases. Since the Middle Ages and up to our own time the Jews in Europe appear to have achieved superior educational and intellectual levels than their analogues in other continents. This is clearly owing to the fact that European countries had a much more advanced cultural milieu than elsewhere. Therefore, to resist the double pressure mentioned above, European Jews had to reach much higher cultural levels than their counterparts in Asia and Africa. The European evolution, especially in the intellectual sphere, was replicated, with variations, in the United States, via European migrations, with the proviso that the favourable attitude of that country towards cultural diversity, whose roots go back to the Pilgrim fathers, rendered less serious the degree of hostility against the Jews. In the United States the Jews organized themselves in a pressure group that is both economically and politically important. The contribution of Jews to the cultural and economic development of the United States should also not be underestimated: their input to technological developments was critical in both civilian and military applications on the eve of the Second World War, when Jews suffered especially massive persecution in Europe, which led to a significant 'brain drain' towards the United States.

In several cultural areas, particularly in the physical and in the social sciences, Jews have been prominent. It is enough to take a look at the list of Nobel prizes, starting in 1901: at least 15 per cent of Nobel prizes have been awarded to Jews, who represent a tiny minority of the world population, no more than 16 million, less than 3 per 1,000.

The way to avoid moving from one type of racism ('Jews are the worst') to the opposite ('Jews are the best') and to try to understand the so-called 'Jewish question' is to generalize that question and to put it in a historical perspective. My view is that the key characteristics of alien groups, and especially Jews, should not be connected to racial (i.e. innate or permanent) differences, but to historical evolution. What history creates, history can cancel out. Empirical support for this view can be found: when in the course of their history alien groups, for whatever reasons, are no longer subject to the double pressure mentioned above, their differences tend to disappear and their characteristics revert to the average.

If my interpretation is well founded, then we have to recognize that the role of Jews and of similar groups has been relevant in the world economic evolution both in former and in recent times. Yet, in certain countries the differences have disappeared or have tended gradually to fade away, owing also to the spread of 'mixed' marriages. In Italy, in the case of Jews, such a process started long ago.

A final remark

Most contemporary economists would consider that the observations presented in this chapter belong not to economic theory, but to sociology, to economic history, to demography and to the field cultivated by that peculiar tribe of economists defined as 'institutionalists'. In a sense, this is so. Certainly, we cannot pretend that theoretical economists should analyse systematically the questions considered in this chapter. Rather, we should hope that they abandon their arrogant attitude in looking to their field as the only one which matters in interpreting social life and adopt a more humble point of view, trying to understand at least the essential analyses of other social scholars and to utilize their results in their economic analysis. The main teaching of Adam Smith, now largely forgotten, is that the different areas of social analysis should not be conceived separately.

3

The inadequacy of mainstream economics to explain development processes: returns and prices

The principle of increasing returns

At this point we are in a position to discuss the growth models worked out by contemporary economists and, in the past, by Classical economists, primarily Adam Smith, David Ricardo and Thomas Robert Malthus.

The fundamental role played by technological and organizational innovations was recognized by Adam Smith, for whom the gradual expansion of the extent of the market promoted the increasing division of labour and thus stimulated innovations and the systematic increase of productivity ('the productive power') of labour: this is what has subsequently been called the 'principle of increasing returns'. The new techniques are embodied in machines, invented or improved by common workmen ('inventing by doing') or, in the case of major innovations, by scientists ('philosophers'). The market expands owing to the growth of traffic and of real incomes, that increase as a result of competition that compels firms almost continuously to introduce innovations to outdo each other, thus pushing down costs and prices.

The Smithian division of labour is often conceived by contemporary economists too schematically, almost trivially, strictly speaking in unacceptable terms. At the very beginning of his *Wealth of Nations* Smith emphasizes that the division of labour can take place either within each firm – this is the case of the famous example of the pin factory – or among different firms. The latter process in turn implies either an increasing variety of intermediate goods for the production of a given final good or an increasing differentiation of similar but not identical final goods, or both. When the division of labour occurs within individual firms, then the size of such firms tends to increase, large firms become more and more frequent and a process of *concentration* takes place; when it occurs among different firms, then we observe a process of *differentiation*. In the various stages of industrial capitalism we observe first the prevalence of a process of differentiation, mainly of intermediate goods, then a concentration process and then again a differentiation process of a new type, mainly referring to consumer goods. The latter is a relatively modern phenomenon occurring after *per capita* income has surpassed the subsistence threshold for increasing masses of persons, so that goods of different varieties capable of satisfying basically the same needs are produced.

The division of labour occurring within individual firms is the origin of economies of scale and, more generally, of what Alfred Marshall called 'internal economies', whereas the division of labour occurring among different firms is the origin of what Marshall defined as 'external economies'; he was emphasizing the importance of localization of productive units in given areas to multiply the spread of this type of economies, consisting in the facility, for firms, to obtain technical and commercial information and intermediate goods and services. To a large extent in a Marshallian industrial district external economies can represent a surrogate for the internal economies of large firms. Referring to Italy, economists of the Bank of Italy carried out an empirical enquiry showing that firms operating in districts obtained net profits between 2 and 4 points higher than profits obtained by similar firms operating in isolation (Banca d'Italia, 1998, p. 85; Baffigi *et al.*, 1999). In chapter 7, I will argue that industrial districts can play an important role in the development of Third World countries.

The main consequence of the division of labour in its various forms is the increase in the productivity of labour owing to the technical and organizational progress made possible. In analysing internal and external economies, Marshall (1949 [1890], book IV, ch. IX) starts with the Smithian division of labour. He was therefore compelled to recognize the importance of technical progress; but such progress was logically incompatible with the static theoretical apparatus that Marshall, such as most economists of his time, had accepted. He could have avoided the contradiction in considering the short-run supply curve of a firm, since in this case plant and technology can be assumed to be given without departing too much from reality. But such an assumption was clearly untenable in the case of the long-run supply curve. To overcome the difficulty Marshall suggested the following: 'We exclude from view any economies that may result from substantive new inventions; but we may include those which may be expected to arise naturally out of adaptations of existing ideas.' Marshall was nonetheless aware of the unsatisfactory character of his solution and remarked: 'such notions must be taken broadly. The attempt to make them precise over-reaches our strength' (1949 [1890], p. 381). While recognizing Marshall's intellectual honesty, we have to point out that the valid answer was not the one that he gave, but would have been to admit quite clearly that a static apparatus is structurally unable to analyse dynamic problems. For logical reasons, time does not and cannot enter into static curves, that are only snapshots, whereas the analysis of dynamic processes requires a moving picture, which consists in an uninterrupted succession of snapshots over the course of time. Single photographs cannot depict movements, even if these are very small. Given the prestige of Marshall and thus his great influence on the economists of his time, he would have done better had he clearly recognized that the introduction of dynamic phenomena into a static system was impossible and that economists willing to analyse technical progress and growth would have to follow another route. To be sure, such a recognition would have implied a drastic departure by Marshall from what was already the dominating paradigm of economic theory.

In spite of his great merits as a theorist Marshall, with his propensity to minimize the logical difficulties arising out of the use of a static apparatus to interpret economic reality, bears the responsibility of having contributed to reinforcing the weight of that apparatus preventing any change in the approach, which would have been very important for analysing the vital problem of growth. Even today we can see the consequences of the unhappy attempt by Marshall to reconcile the Smithian and the neoclassical analyses. In fact, neoclassical economists have accepted both internal and external economies, trying to force them into a static framework; thus they formalized but also sterilized them, cutting the ties – what Marshall tried unsuccessfully to avoid – with Smith's analysis of the division of labour, in which not only time but also space has an essential role. For Smith, the expansion of the extent of the market is a process occurring in the course of time, while the market has a necessary space dimension, of which Smith was fully aware (witness book I, ch. III of the *Wealth of Nations*, 1961 [1776]).

All this has been rediscovered by Paul Krugman (1991), who emphasizes the importance of internal and external economies for understanding the problems of the localization of industry – taking, however, not Smith but Marshall as his point of reference and thus inheriting some of the serious limitations caused by the quasi-static character of the Marshallian analysis.

The principle of diminishing returns

If the origin of the principle of increasing returns is to be found in Adam Smith's analysis of the division of labour, the principle of diminishing returns originates in David

Ricardo's analysis of the distribution of income among rents, profits and wages. In fact, in conducting that analysis Ricardo worked out the principle of diminishing returns with reference to the agriculture of a given country and taking as a starting point Malthus' principle of population. (Ricardo's theory of rent, however, differs from that of Malthus, as Ricardo himself explains in ch. XXXII of his *Principles*, 1951 [1821] but I will not discuss this interesting question here.) Neoclassical economists claim that the principle of diminishing returns can be generalized and applied to individual firms in all sorts of activities; it can be formulated in the following way: 'when a given quantity of a certain factor of production is combined with increasing amounts of other factors, production increases, first, at a rising rate and, after a point, at a declining rate.'

Over seventy years ago Sraffa demonstrated that this generalization does not hold (Sraffa, 1926): the principle of diminishing returns is to be referred, as Ricardo correctly did, to agriculture as a whole, not to individual firms. In a certain country land can be regarded as given, with the proviso that agricultural products of other countries do not enter easily into the country considered owing to transportation costs and, in England at that time, to protective tariffs.

Ricardo recognized that technical progress in agriculture could counteract the tendency towards diminishing returns, but he thought that in practice the 'natural' tendency would have had the upper hand. We know that historically, in the countries that have experienced a vigorous overall process of growth, this has not been the case: owing to technical progress, returns have been increasing in all activities, including agriculture. But the principle as such remains valid. In fact, as we will see, in certain backward countries such as those of Africa South of the Sahara, technical progress in agriculture either does not take place or has not been, and still is not, vigorous enough to offset Ricardo's tendency. (Unlike Ricardo, Smith thought that in a civilized country in agriculture, too, returns were increasing, though more slowly than in manufacturing; for him, particular kinds of diminishing returns could be found in raising cattle and in mineral production.)

If Sraffa is right, then, the principle of diminishing returns cannot be applied to individual firms, neither in agriculture nor in other activities, and in neither the long nor the short run; it follows that, given techniques, marginal cost as a rule is to be seen as constant and therefore coinciding with variable cost in both the short and the long run.

This has been confirmed by a huge amount of empirical studies. Yet, in spite of this and in spite of the devastating critique set out long ago by Sraffa, mainstream economists go on assuming that, as a rule, individual firms' marginal cost curves do not coincide with variable, or direct, costs and that they are both U-shaped. In my view, the reason for this irrational stubborness is not difficult to find: only marginal costs that, at least after a point, tend to increase are compatible with the assumption of perfect competition, an assumption that is still at the foundation of mainstream economic theory.

The marginal cost curve, first decreasing and then increasing, is the counterpart of the marginal productivity curve, related to both individual firms and the economy as a whole. The production curve, too, which is the basis of the marginal productivity curve, is open to radical objections, which I examined elsewhere (Sylos Labini, 1988) and which are relevant in the critique of another pillar of mainstream economic theory, the Cobb–Douglas production function.

The static interpretation of Ricardo's diminishing returns is an aberration, since it arises only when the population is increasing in the course of time and therefore requires the cultivation of lands of decreasing fertility. Smith's increasing returns, too, are inherently dynamic, since they depend on the expansion, in the course of time, of the size of the market. For manufacturing, Ricardo accepted, but did not develop,

Smith's proposition. However, he made an important contribution to the understanding of productivity increases in ch. XXXI, which he added to the third edition of his *Principles*, by establishing a relation between wages and mechanization in manufacturing. Like that of Smith, this proposition, too, is inherently dynamic and, as we will see, can be formalized in an equation including both Smith's and Ricardo's propositions, to explain productivity changes.

Impulses determining the growth of productivity: the productivity equation

The relation between the rate of growth of productivity and that of *per capita* income is very close: given the ratio between the labour force and population and given the distribution of income, the two rates tend to coincide. In its turn, the rate of growth of productivity depends, first of all, on innovations and, secondly, on changes in the composition of output.

The distinction between major and minor inventions is analytically relevant. Major inventions, that give rise to major innovations, are often produced in laboratories of non-profit organizations, such as research institutes and universities. These innovations can have important economic consequences, but they are not determined by profit motives and therefore can be treated as exogenous with respect to the economic system; major innovations of this type have made plausible the idea that all innovations can be considered as exogenous. However, certain major innovations are produced in research laboratories of firms; in these cases, they are determined by profit motives and should therefore be considered as endogenous. Major innovations occur discontinuously, whereas minor innovations take place continuously; for this reason, such innovations have a particularly important role in the growth process. They are conditioned by major innovations and are stimulated by the expansion in the size of the market and by the increase in the relative cost of labour – the former can be defined as the Smith effect, the latter, as the Ricardo effect. These three impulses – innovations produced in research laboratories of firms, the Smith effect and the Ricardo effect – are unmistakably endogenous, since they arise within the economic system. I will concentrate my attention on the endogenous innovations and on manufacturing, which is the most dynamic sector of the economy not only from the standpoint of productivity growth but also because it supplies all sorts of machinery and appliances to the other sectors, including that of high-technology services.

To explain the yearly labour productivity growth in manufacturing by means of an equation, we begin with two variables embodying the Smith and the Ricardo effects. For the Smith effect, we take national income (Y) as an indication of the extent of the market. The Ricardo effect is summarized by his proposition: 'Machinery and labour are in constant competition, and the former can frequently not be employed until labour rises' (Ricardo, 1951 [1821], p. 395); thus, the simplest thing to do is to consider the ratio between wages (W) and the price of machines (P_{ma}) (W/P_{ma}): an increase in this ratio stimulates the substitution between labour and machines. A third variable is aggregate investment carried out by firms, which includes several components, first of all labour-saving (that is, productivity-increasing) investment, which is stimulated by increases of the W/P_{ma} ratio; it then includes also capacity-expanding investment, which is stimulated when demand increases; finally, it includes expenses for building research laboratories and for research and development (R & D). It is not possible to separate the various types of investments; in particular, aggregate investment tends, as a rule, to enhance both productive capacity and productivity, though in different proportions, depending on the relative changes of wages and total demand. In any case, in the productivity equation aggregate investment is lagged and its lag is shorter than the one referring to the W/P_{ma} ratio, since the increase of this ratio stimulates the labour-saving component and therefore presumably the increase of aggregate investment occurs after the increase in that ratio.

We may enlarge our analysis and consider a fourth impulse determining the growth of productivity. Thus wage increases can stimulate not only the introduction of labour-saving machinery (the Ricardo effect), a process that requires time, it can also stimulate the growth of productivity in the short run, quite apart from the introduction of machinery. In fact, when the current increase of wages exceeds the productivity growth already under way – that is, when the cost of labour per unit of output tends to rise – managers are induced to save labour by redistributing jobs among workers within each firm and reorganizing the production process in a more efficient way. If the wage increase is expected to continue at the same speed, managers will be stimulated to introduce labour-saving machines, and here the Ricardo effect becomes relevant. (Alternatively, managers will import intermediate goods produced more cheaply abroad or will transfer their firms, or certain productive operations, to underdeveloped countries, where wages are much lower and increase more slowly. In extreme cases those firms go bankrupt, so that the country considered will begin to import the goods that those firms were producing.)

All considered, the productivity equation is:

$$\hat{\pi} = a + b\hat{Y} + c\,(\hat{W} - \hat{P}_{ma})_{-m} + dI_{-n} + e\,(\hat{L} - \hat{P}) \qquad (3.1)$$

where Y is income, W the wage rate, P_{ma} the price of machines, P the price level, $L = W/\pi$ the cost of labour of output and I the aggregate investment; m and n indicate lags $(m > n)$ and the circumflex accent (ˆ) represents a rate of change. I presented this equation in 1983 (Sylos Labini, 1984); I tested it empirically with reference to various countries, including the United States, where it explains satisfac-

torily the much-debated 'puzzle' of the productivity slowdown, that I will consider in a moment.

The Ricardo effect, embodied in the second variable
$(\hat{W} - \hat{P}_{ma})$, has not been discussed in recent times. Yet, it is
curious to notice that three American economists – Romer,
De Long and Summers – in a departure, at least for this
problem, from the neoclassical paradigm, have partially
rediscovered the Ricardian proposition. Romer concentrated
his attention on wages, while the other two economists, in a
paper written together, concentrated their attention on the
prices of machines (Romer, 1987; De Long and Summers,
1991). I say 'partially', since these economists consider either
the behaviour of wages or that of the prices of machines and
not, as one should, the two variables together; I also say 'partially' because the Ricardian variable is only one of the variables that, in my judgement, are to be used in trying to
explain productivity changes. I remind the reader that Romer
considers not nominal but real wages (W/P) and De Long and
Summers consider the real price of machines, that is the ratio
between the nominal price and the deflator of the gross
domestic product (GDP). Romer considers the long-run behaviour of real wages to interpret the long-run behaviour of productivity and, in particular, to explain the slowdown of
productivity growth occurring in the United States between,
approximately, 1977 and 1982. It is worth observing that the
behaviour of real wages largely corresponds to the behaviour
of the fourth variable of my equation, where I consider not
wages but the cost of labour per unit of output. On the other
hand, the behaviour of real wages also has a certain correspondence with that of the second variable of my equation
$(\hat{W} - \hat{P}_{ma})$, which, however, is lagged. The correspondence is
greater the closer is the behaviour of prices in general, or of
the cost of living, to that of the prices of machines. Often,
however, the correspondence is not close. In any case, it is
more logically correct to compare the behaviour of wages

with that of the prices of machines rather than with the behaviour of the cost of living or of prices in general.

After a painstaking cross-section analysis, De Long and Summers conclude that the relative prices of machines, conceived as the ratio between those prices and the GDP deflator, can greatly contribute to explaining the differences in the levels of productivity in many countries, including several underdeveloped ones.

The basic idea of the three economists is well founded, but wages should be related to the prices of machines and not to the cost of living and the prices of machines should be related to wages and not to the GNP deflator; moreover, as I have already observed, there is not one explanatory variable, but at least four. In particular, Romer intends to present a 'crazy explanation' of the productivity slowdown in the United States; if we take into account just the proposition put forth by David Ricardo, all the 'craziness' disappears; in its place we find an appalling lack of knowledge by the classical economists.

It is more to the point to clarify the Ricardo effect $(W - P_{ma})$. Ricardo maintained that in North America the introduction of machinery was bound to be slower than in England since wages were low and stable owing to the cheapness of food (Ricardo, 1951 [1821], p. 395). As is now evident, Ricardo was utterly wrong, even considering the time at which he expressed that view, which was in sharp contrast with the view by Smith expressed several decades earlier. Ricardo's view was the corollary of his theory of wages, which linked wages almost exclusively to the price of food, whereas Smith had a much richer theory of wages. For Smith, the price of food is certainly relevant, but so is the demand of wage earners, a demand that at that time in North America was interacting with a relative scarcity of labour, owing to the availability of free land (see p. 37 above); this gave rise to an upward pressure of wages, that stimulated the introduction of machinery and of other devices to push up productivity growth more than in England and other European countries. Smith is Ricardo's Virgil in his voyage in the inferno of the economy; but Ricardo does not always follow him, and at least in one important case (the question of the corn standard) he does not even correctly understand Smith's ideas.

The 'law' of supply and demand and prices

In neoclassical theory the so-called 'law' of supply and demand is expressed by two curves, representing a syntheses of hypothetical possibilities, independent of time. In this sense, those curves are static. The demand curve is descending, following the behaviour of marginal utility, and the supply curve is rising, owing to diminishing returns. In a competitive market the equilibrium price is determined by the intersection of the two curves. The characteristic vice of the neoclassicists is to try and explain variations of a given phenomenon occurring over the course of time by assuming shifts in the static curves. This has been done in the case of price variations; but an assumption is not an explanation and the analysis remains static in spite of the shifts.

We must conceive supply and demand not as hypothetical quantities represented by curves, but as *variables changing over the course of time*. In the short run supply is represented by the available quantities, which can be modified to some extent by variations of stocks and output, provided there is unused capacity, while demand is represented by the purchasing power that is directed towards the relevant good. However, the flow of purchasing power is not a datum but a variable, itself depending on price; the same is true for supply to the extent that, in the short run, it can vary; in its turn, price depends on both demand and supply. We thus face a problem of interaction of three variables: price, demand and supply; we can solve this problem with a simple system of three equations:

$$P = a + bD - cS \qquad (3.2)$$
$$D = d - eP \qquad (3.3)$$
$$S = f + gP \qquad (3.4)$$

Price, then, depends on demand and supply in the short run, whereas in the long run it tends towards total cost per unit plus a margin of profit necessary to induce the producers to remain in the market. All this applies to markets under competitive conditions, in which single producers are not able to influence prices. If, owing to variations of supply and demand, price rises above the level of cost plus the profit margin, then new firms enter into the market and price declines, whereas if price falls below that level, inefficient firms leave the market: as a result, in the long run, price tends towards cost. In the long run, however, if demand expands systematically, the techniques of production improve, labour productivity increases and total cost per unit diminishes, provided that nominal wages remain stable or increase less than productivity: this was Smith's point of view. For Smith, productivity tends to rise both in manufacturing and in agriculture, but in the former more than in the latter.

During the most part of the nineteenth century Smith's expectations were fulfilled and the prices of both industrial and agricultural products declined; but the former fell more: the index of finished products in the United Kingdom fell from 100 in 1800 to 22 (!) in 1897; the index of raw materials prices fell less – from 100 to 37 (Sylos Labini, 1993b). The indexes referred to are those of the export and import prices of the United Kingdom; in the nineteenth century, as is well known, the majority of British exports consisted of industrial products, whereas imports consisted mainly of agricultural and mineral raw materials. On the whole, the ratio between the two categories of prices – that is, the UK terms of trade – fell. The fall, however, lasted until the early 1880s, since in the last two decades of the nineteenth century the trend was in favour and no longer against industrial products. In the twentieth century the trend of the terms of trade has, on the whole, been in favour of industrial products.

The question is important because the behaviour of the UK terms of trade can be seen as representative of the behaviour of the terms of trade between industrialized countries and underdeveloped countries, particularly those specializing in the production of raw materials. We are entitled to assume that labour productivity has increased markedly more in industrialized than in underdeveloped countries in both the nineteenth and twentieth century. If this is so, why in the twentieth century has the trend in the terms of trade no longer varied in favour of raw materials, as it did until the end of the nineteenth century, but has moved against them? My answer is that price and wage mechanisms have changed. In industry and services the competitive mechanism, the one described by Smith and Ricardo, has gradually been substituted by a non-competitive one, as a consequence of the process of concentration of firms and differentiation of products. The former has created large firms and generated types of concentrated oligopoly, whereas the latter has given rise to various types of differentiated oligopoly, driven mainly by the increase in *per capita* income; differentiated oligopoly is to be seen as a more precise description of that market form that most economists define as 'imperfect competition'.

In the final analysis, the break in the trend of prices occurring towards the end of the nineteenth century is to be related first of all to the new wage mechanism that, first in Great Britain and then in other industrial countries, was conditioned by the modern trade unions organized in the early 1890s (see Hicks, 1932, ch. XIII). The formation of trade unions was favoured by the process of concentration of firms, that gave rise, in large firms, to regiments of workers. Subsequently, the upward push of wages was fed by the process of differentiation, that affected the market power of both workers and firms no less than the process of concentration. As a consequence firms could, within certain limits, shift onto prices the increases in the cost of labour, even if the other costs did not vary.

In agriculture, where concentration is low and differentiation largely absent, the competitive mechanism is still working; in non-agricultural activities, on the contrary, the competitive mechanism has been gradually substituted by what has been defined as the 'full cost principle' but should be more properly called the 'mark-up' or the 'cost-plus principle'. In the short run price, apart from agriculture, no longer depends on the interaction of demand and supply but on the variation of costs: price is varied together with costs and demand variations are met by changing supply – in the case of an increase in demand, supply can quickly be increased by making recourse to stocks or to imports or to unused capacity. Naturally, in all markets demand and supply interact, but in competitive markets their interaction affects price, whereas in non-competitive markets demand changes affect supply: price depends on cost – and, particularly, on direct cost, given by the cost of wage labour (production workers) per unit and by the cost of intermediate products, energy and raw materials. Direct cost, which is the basis of the mark-up principle, can be considered constant with respect to output and therefore equal to marginal cost, since diminishing returns do not apply to individual firms. If direct cost were not constant with respect to output, the mark-up principle would not be applicable. At the same time, this principle is meaningless in those markets where producers have no influence on price; more important, the principle is meaningless in a static framework since, given oligopolistic interdependence, it is a method to restore immediately a price acceptable to all firms when the elements of direct costs vary. In short, the mark-up principle is meaningful only in a *dynamic context*.

The mark-up principle can be expressed by the relation

$$P = v + qv \tag{3.5}$$

where q is the mark-up and v is the direct, or variable, cost and is equal to the sum of labour cost per unit and the cost of inputs – raw materials, energy and intermediate goods; in a first approximation, we may consider only raw materials, M; the wage cost per unit is given by the ratio between the hourly wage rate and hourly productivity, $L = W/\pi$. Thus, we have

$$P = (1 + q)(L + M) \tag{3.6}$$

The mark-up $(1 + q)$ aims to cover overhead cost per unit at the 'normal' level of output and to give a profit margin – the overhead costs being determined by yearly capital expenses and expenses for general administration, including salaries.

By taking as the mark-up $\mu = 1 + q$, we have

$$P = \mu L + \mu M \ (I) \tag{3.7}$$

Given that the mark-up principle is meaningful only in a dynamic context, to check whether the mark-up remains constant or varies when the elements of direct cost vary, we can use the relation

$$\hat{P} = \mu \hat{L} + \mu \hat{M} \tag{3.8}$$

where the circumflex accent (^) indicates, as before, a rate of change.

The empirical tests that I conducted for several countries, and systematically for Italy and the United States, show that the mark-up is not constant: the shift of cost variations on prices does occur, in one year or less, but it is partial and asymmetrical and follows, though irregularly, an anti-cyclical pattern. This is not the place to go deeper into this matter (Sylos Labini, 1979).

In the long run prices tend to become equal to costs in both competition and oligopoly; but the fact that, in oligopoly, prices depend on costs even in the short run affects also their long-run behaviour, because in our own time the cost of labour per unit of output, which represents more than half of direct costs, very seldom falls – more often it increases, owing to the increased market power of workers, depending on factors such as trade unions and on differentiation occurring in labour markets. Thus, if demand falls but the cost of labour increases, price does not decrease or may even increase; it could fall only if raw materials prices decreased to such an extent as to more than offset the increase in labour cost – a rather rare occurrence. As a final outcome of the structural changes that we have just mentioned, the trend of the prices of industrial products, that in the nineteenth century was sharply falling, has on the whole in the twentieth century has been increasing, more or less rapidly; and this is true even if we neglect wars. In recent years in advanced economies industrial prices have often been relatively stable and even then consumer prices, that include retail trade margins, tariffs, rents and services, have increased, though at a low rate (say, 1.5 per cent per year). The years of the Great Depression appear to be an exception, since all prices fell substantially. But the exception is only apparent, since the prices of raw materials, especially agricultural raw materials, fell dramatically (50 per cent from 1929 to 1932 in the United States), and the fall of the price of finished products, which was much less – 20 per cent – is, in contrast with traditional theory, imputable, not to the fall in demand but to the fall in the prices of raw materials. In the same period in the United States agricultural production remained approximately stable, whereas industrial output fell considerably – by 40 per cent. This is impressive evidence for the fact that demand affects mainly prices in competitive markets (raw materials) and supply in non-competitive markets (industry): here prices are affected by costs. The violent fall of raw material prices affected the whole world and therefore also the other great economy, that of Great Britain; the terms of trade increased by almost 50 per cent against the raw materials themselves (Martin and Thackeray, 1948).

4

The inadequacy of mainstream economics to explain development processes: distribution and growth

The 'price of capital'

Neoclassical economists consider 'capital' as an aggregate quantity that can be measured independently from income distribution, and the rate of interest as its 'price'. This is wrong: 'capital' cannot be measured in that way (compare Harcourt, 1972) and the rate of interest, as Schumpeter pointed out long ago (1934 [1911]), is the price of the loans needed by firms to buy all the means of production, both durable and non-durable capital goods and those constituting the so-called 'circulating capital' – not only intermediate goods, raw materials and energy, but also the services of labour. It is true that durable capital goods – say, machines – require a long period (several years) before the sums of money that have been expended to purchase them can be recouped, whereas those spent on non-durable capital goods and for wages will be recouped in a shorter period (a year or so); it is also true that the interest rate for long-term loans seldom coincides with the short-term rate. As a consequence, a variation of the rates of interest is likely to modify the profitability of the use of the different factors of production and therefore modify the composition of demand of these factors. But we cannot predict whether an increase in the interest rate will reduce the demand for machines relatively to that of labour. Instead, we can certainly state that the demand for machines will increase and that of labour will relatively decrease if wages rise with respect to the prices of machines – which is exactly what Ricardo pointed out. Moreover, we can state that an increase in the rate of interest, *ceteris paribus*, will depress the demand for all sorts of factors of production. However, we can say nothing about the change in techniques, becoming more or less capital-intensive depending on the variations of the interest rate, in complete contradiction to the neoclassical view, according to which there is an inverted relation between the interest rate and the intensity of capital.

The whole question has been reconsidered from a different angle by Piero Sraffa in his *Production of Commodities by Means of Commodities* (1960), and developed by Luigi Pasinetti (1966) and other economists, notably Pierangelo Garegnani (1966). For a period a hot debate took place over the 'reswitching of techniques', meaning the lack of an unequivocal relation between interest and 'capital'. In fact, Levhari (1965), following a suggestion by Samuelson, tried to demonstrate that Sraffa's conclusion was valid, not in general, but with reference only to an individual commodity – a purely abstract case, with no practical relevance. Pasinetti was the first to demonstrate that the 'Samuelson–Levhari theorem' was wrong and that Sraffa's conclusion was generally valid; Samuelson himself promoted a symposium on this question and honestly admitted that the analysis worked out by Sraffa and developed by Pasinetti was well founded (Samuelson, 1966). From the standpoint of logic, then, the victory was for the 'heretics', but mainstream economists have tried to relegate their conclusions to the area of paradoxes in order to save the dominating paradigm. Up to now, this operation has been successful and the debate on reswitching has simply been ignored.

Neoclassical economists consider the substitution between 'capital' and labour that is supposed to occur when, given technology, the ratio between the interest rate – the 'price of capital' – and the wage rate varies. Very different indeed is the substitution determined by a change occurring over the course of time in wages with respect to the prices of machines; thus, if wages rise, new machines will be produced capable of saving labour and these machines will substitute a number of workers. Then, the change in the wages/prices ratio of machines determines the adoption of new techniques. It is thus fitting to call 'static' the neoclassical substitution (changes in relative prices, constant technology) and 'dynamic' the wages/machine price type of substitution. This distinction plays an important role in the critical discussion of another pillar of mainstream economics, the Cobb–Douglas function.

Dynamic and static substitution: a critique of the Cobb–Douglas production function

This function, first developed by Wicksell (1934 [1901–6]) and then rediscovered by Douglas in collaboration with Cobb (Douglas, 1934), was originally intended to explain the distribution of income based on the marginal productivity of the so-called 'factors of production' – as an extreme simplification: capital and labour.

The Cobb–Douglas function is based on the concept of *static substitution*: given alternative techniques to produce a given amount of output, the choice depends on the relative prices of the two factors, capital and labour.

Two preliminary questions arise: (1) whether it is correct to compare, for the choice of techniques, wages and the interest rate and (2) whether it is correct to assume that, at a given point in time, several techniques are available. To the first question the answer is 'no', the correct comparison is between wages and the price of machines. To the second question the answer is 'yes', assuming a given target of output, we can admit that more than one technique be available, but the choice is very restricted. The reason is that wages seldom go down; more often, they go up. When wages fell to a lower level already experienced in the past, firms may decide to revert to a more labour-intensive technique formerly used; when wages go up and reach a level never experienced before, then new labour-saving techniques not yet available are invented or produced by using projects prepared by engineers but not yet carried out. Static substitution is thus of modest relevance, whereas dynamic substitution – the introduction of new technologies – is much more important, not for the number of technologies among which to choose to produce a given output (a number limited in any case), but for the increased productivity of labour made possible by the new technique. On the other hand, the choice of techniques depends not only on the prices of factors but also on the size of firms. In spite of all criticisms, the Cobb–Douglas function has not been abandoned and is still widely used not only with reference to the problems of income distribution but, more and more often, with reference to the problem of the growth process, in both advanced and underdeveloped countries. Even economists recognizing that the criticisms advanced must be taken seriously have defended the Cobb–Douglas function on the grounds that, empirically, it works.

I have criticized the very foundations of this function both in its original version – as a theory of distribution – and in the version conceived as a starting point to explain both income distribution and economic growth (Sylos Labini, 1995b). Here I recall only the essential lines of my critique.

The Cobb–Douglas function is represented by the relation

$$Y = AL^{\alpha}K^{\beta}$$

where Y is aggregate production, A is a constant, L and K represent labour and 'capital' respectively, and the two exponents express the two distributive shares. The Cobb–Douglas function is based on the following assumptions:

(1)   The static substitution between labour and capital depends on the changes in the ratio wage rate/rate of interest.

(2)   Conditions of atomistic competition obtain in all markets, so that prices are parameters.

(3)   Cost curves are U-shaped and all firms are at the point of minimum cost, where, for an instant, returns are constant: only with constant returns is the sum of the two exponents, for labour and for capital, equal to one and Euler's theorem can be applied.

(4)   The various capital goods are malleable and adaptable at will, so that the aggregate capital can be treated as though it were a single capital good (capital being such as jelly).

(5)   The notion of marginal elasticity of substitution, based on the marginal productivity of each factor and often assumed to be constant, allows us to use the exponents of the two factors, L and K, to explain the two main distributive shares.

(6)   The isoquant, expressing the static substitution between labour and capital, is pushed to the right by technical progress, that is assumed to be 'neutral', so that the shape of the isoquant does not change.

(7)   The value of aggregate capital can be measured independently of its returns.

Assumptions (1) and (7) are logically unacceptable; all the others are completely divorced from reality.

In my (1995b) paper, I showed that the success of empirical testing of the Cobb–Douglas function is an illusion. Cross-section testing, as demonstrated by Phelps Brown (1957), does not count; instead, time series are relevant, on condition that the constraint $\alpha + \beta = 1$ be not introduced; but only in very few cases do these tests give favourable results.

Originally the Cobb–Douglas function was intended to explain only the distribution of income. Robert Solow (1956) enlarged it to explain growth of output and productivity as well as income distribution; to this end he introduced a multiplying factor related to time and expressing shifts of the function. It thus became natural to distinguish between movements along the function, depending on changes of the relative prices of factors, given techniques, and shifts of the function, depending on change of techniques. The idea of introducing, by assumption, technical progress by means of a multiplying factor is certainly a brilliant idea, but an assumption is not an explanation. Moreover, before discussing whether it is convenient to keep or to give up the distinction between movements and shifts of the function, we have to face the question of its logical validity, that defenders of the Cobb–Douglas function tend carefully to ignore. If it is true that capital cannot be measured independently of income distribution, then that distinction is meaningless, as is the 'residual factor' to be attributed to 'technical progress' in explaining the growth of productivity (see Arcelli, 1962, 1967; Sylos Labini, 1995b, p. 498).

A further question arises: if the whole analysis, both theoretical and empirical, concerning the Cobb–Douglas function is meaningless, does it represent a complete waste of time? My answer is 'no': in certain respects the analysis can be utilized, on condition that its interpretation is radically changed. Such an interpretation is strictly related to the productivity equation that I presented earlier. The ratio Y/L is a way to consider the productivity of labour of the whole system, or of manufacturing, if we restrict our analysis to this important sector; the ratio K/L in this case is what Pasinetti (1981) defines as the 'degree of mechanization'. The variations of the two ratios are similar, but they do not coincide. The comparison between the two variations can be made with the following formula

$$Y/L = \gamma\, K/L \tag{4.1}$$

It is interesting to notice that the Cobb–Douglas function, under certain assumptions, reduces to (4.1). Indeed, the original function

$$Y = AL^{\alpha}K^{\beta} \tag{4.2}$$

becomes

$$Y/L = \beta K/L \tag{4.3}$$

by putting $A = 1$ and introducing the constraint $\alpha + \beta = 1$. If we abandon the idea of using the Cobb–Douglas function to explain the distribution of income, then the meaning of that function changes completely. In fact, I consider the exponent in (4.3) to be related to the main impulses included in the productivity equation – that is, the Smith and the Ricardo effects. To avoid confusions I call γ the exponent of (4.3). We have then

$$\gamma = a + bY + c\, W/Pma \tag{4.4}$$

My radically revised interpretation of the Cobb–Douglas function has been tested by a distinguished Italian economic statistician, Franco Giusti (1996), who considered a series of individual Italian industries; the results of his inquiry proved to be decidedly favourable to the model expounded here.

The Cobb–Douglas function also continues to be accepted as a sort of dogma in recent works concerning both advanced and underdeveloped countries, often attributing to the exponents more meaning than the original ones, often to try and take into account the currently fashionable concept of human capital. If that function is misleading, as I believe, then its adoption has negative effects in the interpretation of the growth process, since it can divert the analytical efforts of the economists into false directions.

Two essays have now been published on the neoclassical theory of growth and distribution, the former by one of the main exponents of that theory, Robert Solow (2000), the latter by one of its most important critics, Luigi Pasinetti (2000): the two essays are of great interest and can contribute to opening the door to a reappraisal of the critiques of the neoclassical theories that do not include only the models of growth and distribution and that, although significant and radical, have up to now been not so much confuted as simply ignored.

The distribution of income

If the explanation of distribution based on the Cobb–Douglas function is untenable, then we have to work out a valid alternative. In my judgement, the most promising approach is the one proposed more than 60 years ago by Michal Kalecki (1971 [1938]), who refers to manufacturing industry and takes as a starting point the mark-up principle. Some years ago I in fact tried to develop Kalecki's idea from both the theoretical and the empirical point of view (Sylos Labini, 1979). This approach has the advantage of building a bridge between the variations in income distribution and in those of the prices of finished goods and of raw materials; it also has the advantage of taking into account productivity increases and the role, in the distribution of income, of changes in raw materials prices – the role of the changes in productivity is essential in the growth process, that of raw materials in international relations.

From the price equation I presented on p. 75 above, that is

$$P = \mu W / \pi + \mu M \tag{4.5}$$

we get, by multiplying both terms by X, total output, and subtracting from both terms M, raw materials prices, under the assumption that raw materials are imported (M includes also energy and intermediate products)

$$Y = \mu W_T + \mu M X - M X \tag{4.6}$$

and

$$W_T/\ Y = 1/\mu - (M/D_F)\ \mu^* \qquad (4.7)$$

where $PX - MX = Y$ is the industrial value added, $P - M = D_F$ is the deflator of that value and $\mu^* = (\mu - 1)/\mu$; W_T/Y is the share of wages and the share of profits is

$$G/Y = \mu^* P/D_F - C_O Y \qquad (4.8)$$

where C_O represents the overhead costs, given by total salaries, depreciation and indirect taxes.

Since μ and μ^* vary in the same direction, the share of profits rises when μ rises – μ can be seen as an index of industrialists' market power; if we consider the industrial sector in isolation and wages as the only incomes different from profits, then it appears that this market power can be used either by pulling up prices or by pushing down wages. Remembering that $G + W_T = Y$, then the share of profits is inversely related with that of wages. The share of profits is inversely related also with that of overhead costs, most of which are given by managers' and clerks' salaries. It should be noted that in many large companies a fraction of profits becomes a bonus payment to managers, especially top managers. Such bonus payments, as well as the compensation of top managers, reflect the market power of companies.

Some economists, referring to estimates worked out by statisticians, have emphasized that the share of labour in income in the long run appears to be relatively stable; however, if the labour share includes both wages and salaries, then this statement is inaccurate, since the logic and the behaviour of the two types of income are different. On the other hand, if it is true that in the long run the two great income shares – labour and non-labour – have not changed much, this depends mainly on the fact that profits, constituting the main part of non-labour income, cannot decline for very long without originating a crisis. (Paradoxically, however, as we will see in a moment, a crisis may also be the consequence of a prolonged increase of profits.)

From (4.7) above it appears that the share of wages W_T/Y is inversely correlated with the prices of raw materials (and of other inputs). This correlation expresses a conflict of interest between industrial workers and producers of raw materials, which advanced countries often import from underdeveloped countries. Then, when the prices of raw materials decline with respect to those of finished goods, the conflict between industrial workers and industrialists lessens, since both can improve their position at the expense of the countries producing raw materials; when the prices of raw materials rise, social tensions become more acute. At the same time, since raw materials and energy represent important parts of the prices of finished goods, these prices tend to rise owing to the rise of raw materials costs; as a consequence wages tend to rise and a price–wage–price spiral is put in motion. In fact, the reduction of inflation and the lessening of social tensions that until recently occurred in advanced countries are to be attributed to a large extent, in my opinion, to the decline in the prices of raw materials and of oil. For continental Europe, this has helped the political process that has brought us to the Euro. (However, at present – Summer 1999 – the prices of raw materials and of oil are again on the rise.)

The above analysis refers to industry, a large part of which is manufacturing, the most dynamic sector of the economy. It is true that in the advanced economies industry today represents a minority share of employment, only 25 or 30 per cent of the total, the greatest part of the remainder being accounted for by services. Yet, if we consider industrial output and measure it at constant prices, no decline occurs – the decline is the consequence of the diminution of the relative prices of industrial products, a decline which, in its turn, depends on the higher increase of productivity in industry with respect to services (Baumol, Blackman and Wolff, 1989; IMF, 1997).

To some extent, the above analysis concerning prices can be applied to private services, the realm of differentiated oligopoly, where in price formation we often find one type or another of a mark-up principle. For certain services, however, this principle cannot be applied and it certainly cannot be applied to public services where, as a rule, the problem refers to the determination and the variation of tariffs; the prices of such services, that consist mostly of wages and salaries, are conditioned by political decisions and indirectly by the market.

Kalecki's model, which is at the origin of this analysis, was highly praised by Keynes (1939); in spite of this, up to now it has had the same fortune as that of all the models lying outside the dominant paradigm: they have been marginalized and ignored, without any attempt to demonstrate that they are wrong.

Kalecki's model refers to industry and to the two great distributive shares, wages and profits. However, it can be extended, with appropriate integration, to the whole private sector, including independent workers operating in productive activities, in trade and in the professions. Then we have the public sector and, finally, the sector including the unemployed, the pathologically employed (in the informal economy) and the unemployable, that to a large extent coincides with Alfred Marshall's 'residuum'. On incomes of retired and of sick people in both the private and the public sector and on incomes of the unemployed, pathologically employed and unemployable persons interventions of public policy have a paramount influence; such interventions are determined not only by reasons of solidarity, but also to curb microcriminality and for other purposes of general interest. Let us not forget that in advanced countries the share of income passing through the public administration is about 40–50 per cent: most of this share goes to public dependants and to welfare expenditure.

If in the study of income distribution we pass from the national to the international level, we face the great question of rich and poor countries. In the final analysis, this is the fundamental question which this book aims to discuss.

As we have seen, the long-run behaviour of the terms of trade has been unfavourable to underdeveloped countries; this behaviour has contributed to a worsening in distribution at the international level – that is, between rich and poor countries. This undeniable fact, however, should not deter us from recognizing that those underdeveloped countries that have been able to start some manufacturing industries and certain agricultural and mineral productions using relatively efficient technologies have more than offset the adverse effects of the variations in the terms of trade. The underdeveloped countries that have not succeeded in starting those productive activities and that, together with the traditional sector where people live at the subsistence level, have a modern sector with mines and plantations – the model worked out by Authur Lewis (1954) – are in a position gradually to improve their general conditions to a significant extent; the companies producing those commodities should be controlled by natives, otherwise many of the advantages will go abroad in the shape of exported profits.

Referring to the England of his time, a relatively advanced country where, however, agriculture was still a significant share of the economy, Ricardo considered income distribution as the central question of economic growth, since the increase in the share of rents, originating from diminishing returns in agriculture, would have determined a fall in that of profits, admitting that the share of wages could not diminish; as a consequence, accumulation would have tended to slow down, eventually coming to a halt. Marx maintained that a progressive fall in the rate of profits, which normally accompanies a fall in the share of profits, would have brought accumulation, and therefore the process of growth, to an end. This possibility, as is well known, has been discussed by several other economists since Ricardo and Marx. But nobody, as far as I know, has discussed the consequences of a *progressive rise of the rate of profits*. And yet it is reasonable to maintain that such a tendency, too, can have very negative effects on accumulation. The capitalist car will certainly stop when the gasoline is lacking, but it can also stop if the gasoline is excessive and its motor chokes. In fact, I have maintained that the most serious of all depressions – that is, the Great Depression which started in 1929 in the United States and had very serious consequences, both economic and political, in several countries – was originated by a progressive and significant shift in income distribution, not against, but in favour of profits (Sylos Labini, 1984, ch. 8).

In the 1920s in the United States, industrial profits were progressively rising because prices were relatively stable and wages were increasing less than productivity. And since total employment was increasing very slowly, the wage bill was also expanding slowly; this was true equally for the incomes of the self-employed. Thus the demand for consumer's goods was increasing slowly and investible funds were directed less and less towards real investment and more and more towards speculative outlets; but a divergence between real and financial outlets cannot go on for long. The shift in income distribution was thus giving rise in the 1920s to large exports of capital, to speculation in real estate and to the violent stock exchange speculation that in the Autumn of 1929 ended up with the Wall Street great crash; in the succeeding years the financial crisis degenerated into the most serious real crisis of capitalism, with a level of mass unemployment never experienced before.

Similar phenomena occurred in Japan, beginning in 1993; the crisis has had very serious repercussions in several Asian countries, including Indonesia and all the so-called 'Asian tigers' except Taiwan, which had deliberately limited the expansion of economic relations with Japan to avoid tensions with China. The principal preconditions of the crisis were

similar: progressive increase of profits, real estate speculation, boom of the stock exchange and a major financial crisis
centred on the banking system, although in Japan the main
variables – profits, stock prices, land prices and capital
exports – showed asynchronies not observable in the United
States before the 1929 slump. The crisis has also hurt South
America and the advanced countries, but not very seriously,
owing to the financial interventions of the governments of
Japan and the United States as well as of the International
Monetary Fund (IMF). In fact, having being halted in time,
the financial crisis did not degenerate into a persistent real
crisis.

The new growth models

The approach intended to explain the distribution of income
adopted by Kalecki and developed by myself is radically different from the interpretation given by the Cobb–Douglas
function, originally worked out precisely for this purpose
and only subsequently used to interpret a process of growth.
A no less radical difference emerges when we compare the
explanation of the growth process that can be developed if
we adopt a classical, and particularly a Smithian, approach
or if we adopt, instead, the approach proposed in recent years
by a group of economists following a neoclassical framework.

   Until recently neoclassical theory was static: real time was
absent, the curves used expressed hypothetical variations
and techniques were given; thus the analysis of a growth
process was precluded, since the idea of assuming shifts of
these curves for analysing such a process cannot be accepted.

   Works by Romer (1987), Lucas (1988) and Rebelo (1991)
opened the doors to new theoretical developments; the
important book by Barro and Sala-i-Martin (1995) sum-
marizes these and other works, and added original contributions. The neoclassical theory was not rejected, but efforts
were made to pass from a static to a dynamic approach and

to make endogenous the forces pushing for growth. Thus, we can speak of a 'modified neoclassical approach' or of the 'new growth models'.

I do not think that the efforts of these economists have been successful. My main theoretical objection is that, in spite of amendments and integrations of various types, all accept Cobb–Douglas functions. But this function cannot be accepted, as I said, not only because it is based on utterly unrealistic assumptions, but also because two of those assumptions – that the interest rate is the price of capital and the quantity of capital can be taken as given independently from its income – are logically untenable. Those economists treat the Cobb–Douglas model as an unchallenged truth, so that, when Romer (1987) finds that 'the exponent relating to labour can be substantially inferior to its share of income, possibly 0.1 or 0.2', he limits himself to speaking of a 'puzzle'. His conviction that the Cobb–Douglas model is valid is so deeply rooted that it does not occur to him that that finding simply depends on the fact there is something radically wrong with the very conception of that function – dogmas, evidently, cannot be called in question.

Yet, Paul Douglas himself was not so dogmatic. He was so impressed by certain criticisms as to write (1967, p. 178): 'Ragnar Frisch [presumably: Frisch, 1965, chs. 5–7] and Horst Mendershausen [1938], as I remember, said that our study should be thrown in the waste basket and all future research on it discontinued.' Phelps Brown, too, was very critical of the Cobb–Douglas function. For him, the empirical tests based on cross-section comparisons were meaningless and only those based on time series were relevant – not, however, in the sense that two exponents could explain the two great distributive shares. He maintained that 'each exponent simply explains a relationship between two different rates of growth' (Phelps Brown, 1957, p. 550). In my judgement this view, similar to that of Mendershausen, is correct, but incomplete, since it does not consider the problem of the forces conditioning the evolution of the different quantities involved. In my article on the Cobb–Douglas function (1995b) I tried to develop precisely this point.

We have to regret that nobody tried to follow up the clues offered by Mendershausen and Phelps Brown. Let us hope that in the near future those criticisms will be the object of discussion, abandoning the method adopted by mainstream economists with respect to the most embarrassing criticisms – simply to ignore them. It is time to recognize that the critical appraisals proposed by Sraffa, Kalecki, Pasinetti, Garegnani and Mendershausen on such fundamental issues as the principles of increasing and of diminishing returns, the 'price of capital', the Cobb–Douglas function and the distribution of income can be accepted or rejected, but not ignored, as up until now has been the case.

To be sure, the economists of the neo-neoclassical approach to growth do not simply limit themselves to developing and enriching the original Cobb–Douglas model, mainly by introducing increasing returns (in a sense, however, different from that envisaged by Smith or even by Marshall). To take into account the forces of technological change and of investment in human capital, they built various special models. In the book on *Economic Growth* (Barro and Sala-i-Martin, 1995 – an impressive piece of work that certainly cost the authors one barrel each of sweat) we find a healthy preoccupation for studying the relations between theory and its factual implications, so that three chapters of the book out of twelve are devoted to empirical analyses that, happily, are largely independent of the theoretical nucleus. This is largely objectionable to me, not only because the theoretical analysis starts with the Cobb–Douglas function, but also because it refers to one-sector models, an approach to be considered as misleading when one intends to consider the process of technological change. As Schumpeter emphasized long ago, that process is necessarily unbalanced and therefore its analysis requires a *multi-sector* model. A dynamic analysis without technical progress, even if it is formally correct, has very limited interpretative power.

As far as I know, none of the economists of the new growth theories has tried to face the contradictory situation in which they find themselves. They accept the basic apparatus of the neoclassical theory, which consists of a variety of static curves, representing syntheses of hypothetical variations, outside real time. But they want to use such an apparatus for dynamic analyses. This can formally be done by assuming shifts of these curves; but, again, an assumption is not an explanation; worse still, such an assumption becomes a cover which hides the lack of an explanation. Another way is to propose specific relations, as for instance those discussed by Romer (1987) – that is, investment in R & D and in research laboratories built with a view to profit. This is certainly a dynamic relation, but it is not explained how it fits with the underlying apparatus. In my productivity equation (on p. 68) I consider, among the explanatory variables, total investment, which includes also the research component; but that equation expresses certainly a dynamic relation – all variables are real, not hypothetical, and occur over the course of time. Moreover, technical progress pushed by the expansion in the size of the market and changes in the relative increase of wages is undoubtedly endogenous, while in the new growth models technical progress is treated as endogenous without presenting convincing reasons – the above-mentioned relation proposed by Romer concerning investment in research appears to be separated from the basic apparatus of the neoclassical theory.

Briefly: the central problem of the neoclassical theory is to clarify the conditions of the optimum allocation of resources – and, in particular, to single out the equilibrium points of the various phenomena analysed by means of static curves; the fundamental aim of the classical economists – including Ricardo – refers to the conditions favouring the growth of the wealth of nations. For certain short-run analyses and for specific economic problems, the neoclassical approach can usefully be adopted. But for the problems of economic development we should go back to the approaches of the classical economists.

5

Economic relations between developed and underdeveloped countries

Innovations and the great sectors of the economy

Technical progress does not affect all economic activities with the same intensity. Some activities – the innovating ones – will be those imparting the strongest impulses to economic changes; others will profit from the innovations emerging in these activities; still others will decline or even disappear owing to competition from the new activities. Thus, the increase of output as well as the changes in employment should be seen as the result of algebraic sums. The very structure of the economic system undergoes, almost without interruption, changes and readaptations, that appear evident when considering not only individual firms, but also whole sectors, such as agriculture, industry and services. In advanced countries, the agricultural sector has undergone deep changes: output has increased, in spite of the fact that employment has declined in both relative and absolute terms. In developed countries, this decline has seldom been the consequence of expulsion of workers decided by landowners or by managers; more often, it has been the result of decisions of workers leaving agriculture attracted by the towns in the conviction that such a move could improve their lot, at least in theory. Emigration from agriculture imparted an upward push to agricultural wages, thus contributing to determining in agriculture the Ricardo effect – dynamic substitution of machines for labour.

If in the agriculture of advanced countries employment has progressively shrunk as a consequence of migrations from the countryside to the towns and of technical progress, in industry the gradual redistribution of workers among firms and branches has not implied a reduction of total employment, which up to a point increased. Only in the last twenty years in several countries has that redistribution brought with it a reduction in industrial employment and an increase in employment in services. It should be noticed, however, that to some extent the shift is more apparent than real, since some of the workers recorded in industry were supplying specialized services to industrial firms from within and, after leaving, have organized independent units to supply similar services from outside (Momigliano and Siniscalco, 1982). The decline in agricultural employment has been accompanied by such an increase in productivity as to allow an increase in output in keeping with the needs of the population and with the possibilities of exports. A similar process took place in certain sectors of industry. As a rule, the workers employed in the production of agricultural and industrial commodities, or their children, are willing to leave those activities and find a job in services, where often jobs are much less stressful and physically wearing.

The redistribution of workers can take place, and today does take place, not only within given countries but, more and more, also between countries; in this sense, we can speak of an 'international redistribution of labour'. A redistribution of labour can take place within primitive economies, when a new sector starts to develop, attracting workers with wages even slightly higher than the incomes obtaining in the traditional sector. The appearance of a new sector in a given country is in itself an innovation, even if it applies methods and produces goods or services already well known in other parts of the world. Thus, a railway and the consequent collateral effects was an absolute innovation 150 years ago in countries that are today advanced. Today a railway is an innovation – a relative innovation – in an underdeveloped country, say in the centre of Africa. In such a country, the building of a railway represents a break in the routine of the already existing activities. Such an innovation in fact directly or indirectly generates numerous changes in the organization of all other activities.

Technological and organizational innovations, then, imply an unceasing redistribution of workers in both developed and underdeveloped countries and between the two categories of countries. In certain periods the algebraic sum of the redistribution is positive, in others it is persistently negative and employment decreases. Naturally, employment takes on different characteristics depending on the type of country. The governments of underdeveloped countries should be very careful in promoting innovations in traditional activities, such as agriculture and handicraft; in promoting the mechanization of agriculture or the creation of modern factories it is necessary to examine carefully the overall effects and the timing of such interventions.

All things considered, the famous sequence illustrated by Colin Clark (1940) – development first of agriculture, then of industry and finally of services – should not be seen as a sequence primarily conditioned by needs, but as a sequence fundamentally propelled by a great variety of innovations, both important and modest, technological and organizational, that give rise to the process of growth of production and, therefore, to the increase of *per capita* income and to the consequent changes in the composition of the demand for consumption goods. Needs represent passive conditions: they are not dynamic impulses.

The aggregate and multi-sector approaches

If development is inconceivable without technological and organizational innovation, and if innovation necessarily implies a redistribution of workers or of jobs among firms, industries, sectors and even among countries, then the aggregate approach, that can be of some use as a first approximation, becomes misleading if one intends to analyse the process of development, which by its very nature is unbalanced. Keynes himself, the father of the modern aggregate approach, divided the economy into two sectors, as Marx had done long before him: the sector of investment goods and the sector of consumer goods. From the standpoint of development analysis, however, the limitation of the Keynesian approach is that it assumes given techniques and given prices – the change of techniques necessarily implies a change in the system of prices. Even adopting a two-sector model, we must take as variables both techniques and prices.

At one extreme we have Keynes, at the other we find Schumpeter, who was very critical of the aggregate approach some time before Keynes made it standard – for a period the Keynesian theory challenged the prevalence of the microeconomic analysis of mainstream theory. Schumpeter's approach, too, is microeconomic, but it is inherently dynamic. The basic idea is that an entrepreneur creates a new firm to carry out an innovation; if he is successful, a host of imitators follows him, the demand for investment goods expands and this directly or indirectly affects the whole economy, giving rise to a period of prosperity, followed by a period of recession and – though not necessarily – of depression. In other words, for Schumpeter the analysis of the business cycle cannot be separated from the analysis of economic development. In such a framework at the start even a multisector approach is not advisable: we have to begin by considering an innovating firm and then follow through the successive changes in the whole economy. However, when this process has gone far enough, we can examine the sector especially affected by the innovation, which is imparting vigorous impulses to the whole system. This is particularly important when that sector includes the production of the means of production, such as machinery; for the sake of simplicity, we can assume that that sector and the industry producing machinery coincide. Indeed, I long ago (Sylos Labini, 1969 [1956]) developed a model in which the machine sector was carrying out an innovation; since I intended to analyse the consequences of that innovation on total employment and on the system of prices, I realized that a model composed not of two but of three sectors was needed (in working out this analysis I came across Sraffa's prices of non-basic products (Sraffa, 1960), which do not enter, directly or indirectly, into the production of all commodities). When the interpretation of the variations of relative prices is not one of the main purposes of this analysis, we can make use of a model with two sectors: one producing consumer goods, the other investment goods.

We limit ourselves to manufacturing and analyse these two sectors from the point of view of the productivity equation, which we thus split into two equations:

$$\hat{\pi}_c = a_c + b_c \hat{Y}_c - c_c\,(\hat{L}_c - \hat{P}_c) + d_c\,(\hat{W} - \hat{P}_{ma}) + e_c\,I_{-n} \qquad \text{(a)}$$

$$\hat{\pi}_{ma} = a_{ma} + b_{ma}\hat{Y}_{ma} - c_{ma}\,(\hat{L}_{ma} - \hat{P}_{ma}) + d_{ma}\,(\hat{W} - \hat{P}_{ma}) + e_{ma}\,I_{-n} \quad \text{(b)}$$

We assume that the prices of both categories of goods are proportional to the ratio between wages and productivity.

We consider three periods. In the first period, the two sectors grow at the same rate in terms of productivity so that, if employment remains stable, productivity and income increase at the same rate in both sectors. In the second period, owing to an external impulse – for instance, an innovation coming from a non-profit institution – the investment sector grows more rapidly than the consumption sector, then, owing to the Smith effect, π_{ma} increases more rapidly than π_c. In the third period, if W does not vary, the price of investment goods diminishes. Such a decline, owing to the Ricardo effect, gives rise to a further increase in productivity in the investment sector, in a self-reinforcing process. It also generates a productivity increase in the consumption sector, since

this sector also employs machinery produced in the investment sector.

The productivity equation and the increasing competition of underdeveloped countries in manufacturing

Accepting a criterion suggested by Adrian Wood (1994), we
can use a two-sector model similar to the one discussed in the
previous section to begin analysing trade relations between
developed and underdeveloped countries. We consider two
sectors of manufacturing of a developed country: in the first
sector relatively unskilled workers, in the second relatively
skilled ones prevail. The first sector produces goods that
meet the competition of similar goods produced by underdeveloped countries, a competition that, with the progress of
transportation, is increasingly severe, since wages in underdeveloped countries are only a fraction, and sometimes a
small fraction (1/10 or even less) of the wages paid in developed countries.

I characterize the variables of the productivity equation of
sector u, where unskilled workers prevail, with subscript u
and the variables of the other equation with subscript s
(skilled workers):

$$\hat{\pi}_u = a_u + b_u\,\hat{Y}_u + c_u\,(\hat{L}_u - \hat{P}_u) + d_u\,(\hat{W} - \hat{P}_{ma}) + e\,I_{-n} \qquad (c)$$

$$\hat{\pi}_s = a_s + b_s\,\hat{Y}_s + c_s\,(\hat{L}_s - \hat{P}_s) + d_s\,(\hat{W} - \hat{P}_{ma}) + e\,I_{-n} \qquad (d)$$

Examining the interactions among the different variables we
realize that productivity changes are affected by contrasting
forces. In particular, the competition of underdeveloped countries in the sector u – let us call 'traditional' the industries
belonging to this sector, where unskilled workers prevail –
tends to push up imports in the developed country considered
of goods produced by underdeveloped countries and thus to
depress the level or the rate of increase of demand for those

goods that are domestically produced. Owing to the Smith effect this has a negative impact on productivity growth. On the other hand, that competition tends to depress P_u and this stimulates firms of developed countries to push up productivity to avoid being excluded from the market. However, that competition tends to depress the rate of increase of wages, and this, due to the Ricardo effect ($\hat{W} - \hat{P}_{ma}$), tends to depress productivity. All things considered, it seems that in traditional industries the forces pushing up productivity are weaker than the opposite forces, so that in those industries the increase of productivity tends to be less than the average in manufacturing industry. In contrast, in industries of sector s, where skilled workers prevail – for instance, the sector producing machines – it is likely that the self-reinforcing process hinted at in the previous section takes place; we expect, then, a productivity increase greater than average in this sector.

The data in table 5.1 illustrate some of the points just mentioned. They refer to relatively long periods and to Italy, but I believe that the trends that they show, though with significant differences, apply also to other developed countries, especially in Europe. Textiles and shoes are industries representative of sector u, whereas machinery is representative of sector s.

Table 5.1 shows that the expectations concerning productivity, imports and exports are fulfilled. Clearly, when in an advanced country the rate of increase of imports of the products of a traditional industry exceeds the rate of increase of exports, the relative weight of that industry in that country in terms of output and of employment is bound to decline, though very slowly. In Italy, this is the case in the two traditional industries examined.

For employment, it is important to distinguish between dependent and independent workers. Total employment in manufacturing industry tends to decline, but this is owing to the behaviour of dependent workers: the self-employed tend to increase, slightly on the whole, considerably in certain

Table 5.1 *Productivity, imports and exports of certain Italian industries, 1970–1996, average yearly rates of change, 1970 = 100*

	Textiles	Shoes	Machinery	Manuf. industry
1 Production	1.1	0.4	4.7	2.0
2 Productivity	2.0	0.5	3.3	2.7
3 Wages	2.4	3.1	2.2	2.3
4 Imports	2.5	4.2	3.7	1.8
5 Exports	1.7	2.2	5.4	2.2
6 Employment	77	98	92	85
Dep. workers	70	92	90	83
Indep. workers	102	131	119	101

Notes:
1 and 6: 1970–96; 2, 3, 4, 5: 1981–96. dep. = dependent
indep. = independent.
Sources: ISCO, *Quadri della contabilità nazionale italiana,*
1970–1994, (1995), n. 2; ISTAT, *Statistiche del commercio estero.*
For machinery see also United Nations Conference on Trade and
Development (UNCTAD) (1999). For mechanical industry see also
United Nations Conference on Trade and Development (UNCTAD)
(1999).

industries such as shoes. The independent workers, then, react in different ways to the competition of underdeveloped countries. In fact, to defend their independence self-employed workers are more likely to accept a reduction in their income than wage earners – in the latter case owing also to the resistance of trade unions. On the other hand, the activity of independent workers is more resilient than that of the firms with dependent workers and, by differentiating their products, they can more easily find 'niches' in national and international markets. Also firms, to defend themselves against the competitive pressure of underdeveloped countries, tend to intensify the improvement of their product quality: differentiation can act as a particular shelter for those industries. This and other reactions to competitive pressure can slow down the gradual shifts of increasing shares of traditional industries towards underdeveloped countries. Certainly, to meet that competition a progressive reduction of wages and incomes of the self-employed is not conceivable.

However, there are other types of reaction: to profit from the much lower wages in underdeveloped countries some of the firms of the sector can transfer their activities, or part of them, to these countries. When this occurs, the size of such a sector undergoes a further decrease in terms of both output and employment. Tariff protection is to be avoided, since it would give shelter only in the short run and would make things worse in the long run. Those sectors or subsectors where workers with relatively low skill prevail are gradually left to underdeveloped countries, which in the course of time are likely to become less and less underdeveloped and eventually (though not necessarily all of them) to enter into a rapid spiral of development. The economically advantageous protection of advanced countries can be afforded, not by tariffs, but being always at the cutting edge both of pure and applied research in a group of industries. (In Italy, mechanical industry fares relatively well and probably the good performance that table 5.1 shows is imputable to the high-technology subsectors of this industry. In the past Italy's position in the computer industry was very good; today, this is no longer the case. On the whole, both industrialists and public bodies in Italy invest in research much less than in other advanced countries. If this trend is not radically changed, Italian prosperity will be in peril in the long run.)

I have dwelt at some length on the issue of the competition coming from underdeveloped countries first of all to show that a two-sector model, in spite of its simplicity, can help us to understand certain important aspects of the changes generated by that competition which could not be analysed with a one-sector model. But there is another reason.

The analysis based on the model concerning the three

Italian industries illuminates aspects of a process that is common to all advanced economies and that in the long run generates deep changes in the international division of labour in modern industry. This process began long ago in the textile industry, the first to appear in the development of modern capitalism that started in England towards the end of the eighteenth century and then spread to other European countries. It has been estimated that at the beginning of the twentieth century 34 per cent of all the raw cotton, indicating the degree of development of the textile industry, was utilized in Western Europe; in 1989 this share had fallen to 7 per cent, whereas in Asia and Oceania the same share had increased from 7 to 35 per cent. The share of steel processed in Western Europe – an indicator of the degree of development of the metalworking industries – was 45 per cent in 1900 and 19 per cent in 1989, whereas in Asia and Oceania the share rose from 0.3 to 26 per cent. These and other figures estimated by Fortis (1993), indicate gigantic shifts in the international division of labour that take a long time to become fully manifest. Such shifts correspond to the sequence described by Hoffman (1958) occurring during the process of industrialization – traditional consumption goods, certain mechanical products, industries producing higher-order goods; in turn, this sequence largely corresponds to the diffusion of the different degrees of the education of the population in general, and of the labour force in particular.

A final observation. The models here briefly recalled represent very simple examples of the multi-sector approach, in which, however, unlike the Keynesian two-sector model, prices and technology are not given: a multi-sector approach of this type is necessary for analysing a process of growth propelled by technical progress. An approach is needed that is no longer tied to the limitations of a two- or three-sector model; in my view, the approach suggested by Luigi Pasinetti with his analysis of vertically integrated sectors (Pasinetti, 1981) is the most promising one.

The meaning of 'globalization'

By 'globalization' we mean the rapidly increasing economic relations at the world level among individuals, among firms and other organizations and among countries. In the last twenty or thirty years such a process has become much more rapid than in the past, but it started long ago: strictly speaking, it started with the development, in certain European countries, of so-called 'commercial capitalism', from the fifteenth century onwards. In a nutshell, the basic difference between capitalism in its various forms and precapitalistic societies is that the economic life of these societies can be represented by a circle, whereas the capitalist process should be seen as a spiral. A spiral can take place in a given country but, as it unfolds, sooner or later it tends to affect other countries. The capitalist process thus crosses national boundaries, and financial and commercial relations tend to become international.

To fix these ideas, we may consider a firm that at the beginning of a yearly cycle of its activity employs a sum of borrowed money, with the promise of giving back at the end of the year that sum increased by the value of the interest rate. If the loan has been equal to 100 and the rate of interest is 5 per cent, then the firm has to pay back 105 units; if the rate of gross profit has been 9 per cent, then the firm has to give 5 units of its surplus as interest, thus obtaining 4 points as net profit. If net profit is invested, then the following cycle starts no longer with 100, but with 104 and at the end the investor will get more than 109: if a sequence of this type goes on, the circle becomes a spiral.

When loans are given, not to firms, but to families, for their consumption, the rate of interest is paid, not out of profits, but from other incomes: the source of interest is not a surplus originated by the activity made possible by the loan, but an income going to the family independently of the loan. Productive and unproductive loans have always taken place, but in the distant past unproductive loans were the rule and productive loans were the exception. In the last 300 or 400 years the ratio has turned upside down and productive loans have become ever-more important than consumption loans: the spiral has prevailed over the circle – this is an essential trait of capitalism.

At the origin of the process of globalization we have that spiral embracing more and more of the world; the recent acceleration is to be attributed mainly to the development of telecommunications, which have particularly affected financial relations.

Financial, real and human globalization

Financial globalization is much easier to carry out than real globalization, which refers to productive activities, being the result of the changes in the international division of labour. 'Human globalization' implies transfers of groups of persons from certain countries to others or transfers of large masses of persons – that is, migrations.

The first steps of financial globalization can be traced back to certain countries or parts of Europe – such as Holland or certain Italian towns – where commercial capitalism started to develop during the Middle Ages. Both processes of globalization – financial and real – became much more rapid during the development of modern industrial capitalism – that is, during the last 200 years. During the last twenty or thirty years both processes have reached an unprecedented velocity, for two reasons. First, the development of a number of major innovations in transportation – aeroplanes, giant cargo ships – and in telecommunications. Second, an increasing number of countries have overcome the three critical thresholds of a modern process of development: (1) a minimum political stability, (2) a minimum level of efficiency of public administration and (3) basic education for relatively large masses of workers that receive very low wages. In such countries, modern firms appear in industries, such as textiles, established long ago in developed countries and whose productive methods are standardized and undergo only small changes. The productive methods being very similar and wages being considerably lower, these countries are capable of moving more and more severe competition to developed countries.

The process of globalization is affecting not only traditional industries, such as textiles, but also new industries, at least in those areas where standardization of productive operations has been pushed far enough to reduce the difficulties of imitating the original products. In the production of highly standardized products even underdeveloped countries are able to enter successfully into international markets – this has occurred in the field of computers in the case of countries such as South Korea, Taiwan and Malaysia. Naturally, in this process underdeveloped, and even a number of developed countries, are as a rule in a position to imitate or to adapt innovations, but not to produce them, since well equipped research laboratories and an adequate cultural background can be found in only very advanced countries.

Real globalization, then, is a very long process that partly consists in the new firms created by local capitalists taking as models the firms of advanced countries and in the shift of parts of the productive chain or of whole firms from advanced to underdeveloped countries. The consequence is an unceasing redistribution of the international division of labour.

Ricardo developed his theory of comparative costs for explaining international trade in the strict sense, i.e. exchange of commodities, by assuming that factors of production did not move from one country to another – and given techniques. Under such assumptions – non-transferable factors of production and given techniques – resources endowment appeared as a key factor in the international division of labour between countries producing raw materials and countries producing manufactured goods, a division that in this way was theoretically justified.

It is fitting to point out that the assumption of 'given techniques' that Ricardo made in certain cases had a completely different meaning than in neoclassical theory: here this assumption is vital and to try and analyse dynamic problems traditional economists have to have recourse to the device of assuming shifts in their static curves. In Ricardo's analysis there are no obstacles to introducing technical changes; in fact, he does so several times (e.g. Ricardo, 1951 [1821], pp. 36–7) and admits that in agriculture, too, technical progress can offset the 'natural' tendency towards diminishing returns, though in the long run – as a matter of factual judgement and not of logic – it is very likely that the latter tendency will have the upper hand (1951 [1821], pp. 90, 123). It is true, however, that Ricardo does not attribute great importance to technical progress, in particular to that driven by Adam Smith's division of labour; only in ch. XXXI 'On Machinery' does Ricardo treat systematically the consequences of saving-labour machines, but we have to remember that that chapter was added in the third edition of the *Principles*. Thus, of the two main economic forces making for technical progress and for the increase in productivity – i.e. the expansion in the size of the market and the increase in the relative cost of labour – Ricardo studies only the latter and only in that added chapter. Admitting that in the era of globalization the international mobility of all factors is rapidly increasing and that absolute as well as comparative costs change gradually but substantially owing to technical changes, and considering the rise in the degree of education, the international division of labour becomes less and less stable in the course of time. Thus, at the end of the nineteenth century the share of the exports of raw materials of the underdeveloped countries was more than 96 per cent of the total, whereas the share of the exports of manufactures was less than 4 per cent; this share was very little higher in 1950. The great change occurred later and especially in recent years: today that share, for the underdeveloped countries considered as a whole, exceeds 60 per cent (Grilli, 1999, p. 146). This means that the endowments of natural resources have a decreasing importance, whereas human resources and technical knowledge have an increasing importance in conditioning the flows of international trade. It remains true, however, that international relations – including, besides commodities, services, capital movements and migrations of persons – are essential in the process of growth of both developed and underdeveloped countries.

The figures concerning the rising share of manufactures in total exports of underdeveloped countries indicate that the competition that those countries are posing to developed countries in the area of traditional industries is becoming more and more pressing. Developed countries have to be prepared gradually to abandon a great part of their traditional industries, concentrating on certain special sectors of such industries and to expand industries based on new technologies. Naturally, in the long run such industries will become old and will be assumed by less developed countries; but, if research activities go on expanding, new industries will take the place of the old ones (see Quadrio Curzio, 1999).

An increase in the efforts devoted by developed countries in the area of research and development (R & D) benefit not only those countries, but also developing countries, provided these adopt open trading policies. The benefit to the developed countries is deemed to be very large indeed: it has been estimated that, *ceteris paribus*, a permanent increase of 0.5 per cent of GNP in R & D spending in all industrial countries brings about an increase in their potential output of 7 per cent in ten years and 11 per cent in twenty years. On the other hand, an increase in imports of high-tech manufactures by developing countries equivalent to 5 per cent of their GDP raises their output by 9 per cent in the long run (IMF, *World Economic Outlook*, 1997, p. 49). By adopting a completely different approach I compared the rate of change of real R & D spending and the rate of change in real national income in Italy. I found a significant influence of R & D spending on changes in income, with the values of the former variable lagged by three and four years – a reasonable result, since the R & D spending has delayed effects spread out over a relatively large number of years, but the most important effects are likely to be concentrated over a few years.

The figures just mentioned are purely indicative; however, they emphasize that the profitability of investment in R & D is very high indeed, provided a long-run horizon and a national point of view are adopted. This means that the political leaders of the country should be both cultivated and far-sighted.

A warning, however, is relevant: the share of high-tech exports in itself cannot be taken as an index of the degree of technological development of a country. In fact, we have to consider the whole productive chain: if a given country imports many intermediate goods from more advanced countries, that share, if judged from the final goods exported, becomes misleading (Lall, 1998).

All things considered, the progress of globalization implies advantages for both developed and underdeveloped countries; but it also implies an increasing competition between the two categories of countries, in both directions; this stimulates the efficiency of the activities involved, but also provokes losses, difficulties and suffering, that are particularly serious in underdeveloped countries less capable of innovating: to reduce the temptation of having recourse to non-economical protection it is to be recommended that a well devised programme founded on financial and non-financial interventions be agreed between the interested governments and international organizations.

The process of globalization does not necessarily imply a tendency towards equalization: in certain cases, it can bring increasing divergencies.

Migrations and international relations

To some extent, immigration of people from underdeveloped countries to advanced countries can be the substitute for the emigration of firms from the latter to the former, when the managers of firms operating in the advanced countries do not find enough unskilled workers at home with the minimum requisites of education, even if they are ready to pay relatively high wages. In addition to this, we observe today considerable flows of immigrants trying to enter the advanced countries, even when not all of them are welcome; those immigrants leave their mother country to escape political or ethnic persecution, or hunger, or both. In certain advanced countries, this has become a very serious problem.

Migrations from one country to another characterized the early colonizations by European powers. The composition of the emigrants was very different according to country and to period: cadets of aristocratic families in Spain or Portugal bringing with them soldiers and bureaucrats, tending to transplant quasi-feudal institutions to the colonies; adventurers in search of mines of precious metals; people endowed with a non-negligible cultural patrimony who fled their mother country for religious freedom and not for economic motives. These were movements of groups of persons, not at first numerically important. But when we discuss the problem of migrations we as a rule refer to the movements of considerable masses of people, such as those in the nineteenth century of European poor towards the New World – North and South America, Australia, New Zealand – and those of our time, in which Western Europe, in the past a land of emigration, has become a land of immigration.

Despite many problems and suffering, such migrations,

arising not only and often not mainly for economic reasons, have significantly contributed to the change in the international division of labour and to the process of growth of different countries in different ways. We should not neglect the remittances sent to their mother countries by temporary or permanent migrants; these remittances played an important role in the process of growth of Italy in the period from the end of the nineteenth to the beginning of the twentieth century and of Egypt after the Second World War.

A very special type of temporary migration is created by the increasing flow of tourists from advanced countries: indeed, to travel abroad is one of the most important ways to spend a share of an income that now is further and further away from subsistence level for an increasing number of people.

Trends and cycles in developed and underdeveloped countries and the terms of trade

The process of growth of the now advanced countries has its propulsive sector in investment and has proceeded through cycles – a process that has been properly called 'cyclical growth'. Since in underdeveloped countries the investment sector is very limited, or does not even exist, the international process of cyclical growth is largely led by advanced countries. This applies to quantities, mainly through international trade, and to prices, especially to those of raw materials. In fact, in each country the business cycle mainly affects the composition of output and employment in the case of finished products, and prices in the case of raw materials.

Advanced countries produce principally finished industrial products and services; the most developed of such countries produce high-technology products that represent significant shares of both their manufacturing output and their manufacturing exports (United States, 44 per cent; United Kingdom, 40; Japan, 39; Germany, 25; in Italy, it is only 15 per cent. *World Development Report*, 1998–9). High-technology products enjoy a sort of temporary monopoly and in any case are outside the competition which refers to prices. Some of the developed countries produce not only finished products but also raw materials (one of them, the United States, in important quantities). But underdeveloped countries, especially those in which manufacturing industry is very limited, specialize in the production of a few raw materials, both agricultural and mineral.

The behaviour of the economies of middle-income countries shows characteristics common to both the advanced and the underdeveloped countries, with the proviso that in each historical period every great area of the world has had a particular leader – a 'locomotive' – of the growth process.

During the competitive stage of modern capitalism all prices were falling and, until the 1880s, the terms of trade were moving in favour of raw materials, in the sense that the prices of finished products were falling more rapidly than those of raw materials. Then, as we have seen in chapter 3 (p. 73), this trend was reversed, owing to changes in price and wage mechanisms. Today, in very simplified terms, the prices of finished products and of services vary on the basis of the so-called 'mark-up principle', whereas the prices of raw materials vary, fundamentally, in relation to the variations of demand and supply. However, given the importance of the question for underdeveloped countries, it is well to go somewhat deeper into the analysis.

The variations of demand for raw materials depend on those of the industrial output of the advanced countries. However, besides the demand for productive purposes we have the demand owing to speculation. The latter demand, often pushed by supply shocks, can be seen as a function of (1) the expected rate of variation of prices and the short-term rate of interest, which represents the main financial cost of holding stocks, and (2) the expected quotation of the dollar, which is still the main means of payment most generally used in international transactions concerning raw materials. A speculative component in the demand for raw materials is always present, but is more or less important depending on the degree of stability of the international monetary system. Thus, until 1971 – that is, before the abandonment of the Bretton Woods agreements that implied a tie, though indirect and limited, between the dollar and gold – the speculative component in the demand for raw materials was not important, whereas it became very important after 1971. Thus, if we compare the period 1954–70 with the period 1971–97 and consider the prices of raw materials as a function only of the industrial output of the OECD countries – i.e. omitting the supply of raw materials and the financial variables – the coefficient of that index is equal to 0.7 in the first period, whereas in the second it is 2.6, showing that the variability of the prices of raw materials has increased considerably – almost four times – as a consequence of the increased weight of the speculative component of demand (Sylos Labini, 1984, pp. 150–1).

In sharp contrast with the behaviour of the prices of raw materials in international markets we have that of the prices of finished goods – in this case I consider the case of the United States: the former show strong oscillations (−9–+8 per cent in the first period, 1954–70, −18–+28 per cent in the second period, 1971–97, with a peak of +61 per cent in 1973), the latter increase systematically, but those increases are relatively limited until 1972. They become pronounced only in 1974 and 1975 (+15 and +14 per cent, respectively), clearly not as a consequence of demand increases – in those two years a sharp recession took place – but owing to the increase of the elements of direct cost (labour, intermediate products, raw materials and energy; in those years, the prices of energy played the most important role). In the period considered (1954–97), the index of the prices of finished products shows only one decrease, in 1986: the decrease was only 1.4 per cent and was owing to a decrease of the prices of raw materials, not to a diminution of industrial output, which increased in that year.

In general, the relation between prices and demand (even neglecting supply) is clear and statistically significant in the case of raw materials, but in the case of finished products that relation does not exist. Thus, the comparison between the behaviour of the two categories of prices – raw materials and finished products – demonstrates beyond any reasonable doubt that in the short run in competition prices depend on demand and supply, whereas in oligopoly they depend on direct costs that, for the reasons already seen, tend to vary in an upward direction or to remain stable – they seldom fall.

On the whole, in our time the ratio between the prices of finished products and those of raw materials has tended to increase; and this is true not only when considering different countries, but even in the same country – in the United States from 1954 to 1997, that ratio increased by 37 per cent. The gap tends to be higher when considering, on the one side, finished products of advanced countries, where concentrated and differentiated oligopolies are widespread, and workers enjoy a remarkable market power and, on the other, raw materials produced in underdeveloped countries, where competitive conditions are the rule and, in addition, governments can do little to support their prices of raw materials. In fact, the oscillations of the prices of raw materials produced in advanced countries are much less violent than those of the prices of raw materials in international markets, a good share of which are produced in underdeveloped countries, where financial and storage facilities are much less well organized than in advanced countries. In such countries, a price support policy can be successful, putting a limit to the downward variations of the prices of raw materials, especially agricultural raw materials. The gap between the two categories of prices in the long run tends to increase, because the prices of raw materials rise, sometimes considerably, in the ascending phase of the business cycle, when demand increases, but fall when demand is declining, whereas the prices of finished products tend to rise and only exceptionally and insignificantly fall.

The disadvantage of underdeveloped countries does not necessarily become more and more serious, for two reasons. First, there are various types of raw materials and some of them may not be disadvantaged for long periods. Second, some of those countries may gradually develop industrial products, though very simple that, on a lower scale, may enjoy some market power. Moreover in certain underdeveloped countries, such as India, some enclaves of high-technology industries have appeared. On the other hand, as already noted, highly developed countries, such as the United States, produce several raw materials. Probably the main difference between underdeveloped and developed countries lies in the fact that the former have a limited number of goods entering into international markets and a low capacity for creating new production, whereas the latter have a high variety of goods and are able to start new productions continually.

All things considered, the disadvantage of the underdeveloped countries that produce only a few raw materials can be serious and can become more and more serious for a considerable number of years. True, in the ascending phase of the business cycle these countries can enjoy some relief, since the prices of raw materials increase more than those of finished products, including the products that they import. The relief, however, is only temporary. And the negative effects of the fall of the prices of raw materials, occurring in the descending phases of the business cycle, can be particularly serious in two areas: the fiscal revenue of the state and the service of foreign debt. In fact, in underdeveloped countries specializing in the production of a few raw materials a considerable share of fiscal revenue depended directly on the duties imposed by the state on the exports of raw materials; indirectly, the effects can be no less damaging owing to the diminution of incomes of those engaged in such production.

No doubt, the adverse variations of the terms of trade represent an obstacle to growth of underdeveloped countries. But it is not the most important one. The main obstacles are to be found in the historical and cultural evolution – that is, in the social structure of these countries.

6

Demographic pressure and the countries of increasing poverty

Two demographic explosions

Demographers agree that after centuries of oscillations in the populations of the world, with a relatively slow tendency towards an increase, in the nineteenth and the twentieth centuries mankind underwent two demographic explosions, one small and one great. The former occurred in the nineteenth century and affected a limited group of countries that were experiencing considerable economic growth. The latter occurred in the second half of the twentieth century and affected a much larger group of countries that were, and still are, experiencing a slow and discontinuous economic growth – only a few of them are at present entering into a process of sustained growth. To fix these ideas table 6.1 may be useful; the data (in millions) are taken from Livi Bacci (1996), except those of 1800, which are very rough estimates.

The really great demographic explosion thus occurred during the twentieth century and has largely affected 'poor' countries.

Each explosion consists in a process, called a 'transition' by demographers, in which the population increases owing to a decline in the death rate accompanied by a birth rate at first stationary and then declining. When this decline becomes rapid and tends to converge toward the death rate, the increase of population, after reaching a maximum, tends towards zero or to become negative, unless immigration

Table 6.1 *Population change, 1800–2000*

	Total	'Rich' countries	'Poor' countries
1,800	1,000	300	700
1,900	1,630	560	1,070
2,000	6,160	1,190	4,970

blocks or reverses this trend. On the whole, the rate of change of the population follows, in the course of time, a sort of Gaussian curve. In the countries experiencing a sustained process of growth, the rate of change of population started increasing during the Industrial Revolution, reaching its maximum at the turn of the nineteenth century, and declined progressively during the twentieth century, at the end of which in these countries population tended to become stationary.

It is fitting to emphasize that the Industrial Revolution should not be seen simply as an economic phenomenon, but as the expression of a *cultural revolution*: it consisted not only in the application to productive activities of important inventions – first of all the steam engine – but also in the spread of hygienic and medical knowledge and in the building of public works such as aqueducts and sewerage, aimed at improving the general hygienic conditions of the population, and in consequence reducing the incidence of infectious diseases. These are the causes of the decline in the death rate, a decline also promoted by the increasing availability of food, and subsequently driven by improvements in medical techniques and by innovations in pharmaceutical chemistry.

The decline of the birth rate was determined by different factors. The spread of economic welfare, which is the consequence of growth, as a rule reduces both fertility and natality, for various reasons that we will consider shortly. The hypothesis can be suggested that the decline of the birth rate became more and more rapid, thus tending to approach the death rate, at the turn of the nineteenth century because in that period in the advanced countries economic welfare began to affect an increasing number of people – to give only one instance, trade unions became socially relevant institutions.

The process of 'transition' is determined by the gap between the two rates depending on different factors: the birth rate depends on the level of *per capita* income and on other socio-economic factors, whereas the death rate depends on hygienic conditions and on medical and pharmaceutical innovations. In the final analysis, however, economic development, driven by a process of cultural development, conditions in various ways the factors affecting the behaviour of both birth and death rates.

The demographic evolution of underdeveloped countries presents certain features that are similar to those of the advanced countries, and others that are different. A similar feature was that in both types of countries populations remained largely stationary for centuries, or only very slowly increasing, since a high birth rate – even 50 per 1,000 or more – was matched by a death rate of comparable magnitude. There were, it is true, violent oscillations owing to wars, famines and other calamities as well as to invasions and migrations. A very important difference between the now advanced countries and the still underdeveloped ones is in *timing*: in underdeveloped countries that as a rule, after the great geographical discoveries, were colonies of the more advanced ones, populations began increasing at a sustained rate much later than in the advanced countries, owing to a decline in the death rate that started only at the beginning of the nineteenth century. The decline, so it seems, was very slow, much slower than that occurring in the advanced countries. The fact is that in these countries the demographic explosion was originated by internal factors, whereas in the underdeveloped countries it was caused by external factors: it was determined mainly by the impact of advanced countries. For a long period, however, the impact on the death rate was very slow.

The Industrial Revolution represented a watershed also in the underdeveloped countries. Indeed, after the great geographic discoveries and before the Industrial Revolution, colonies were important for strategic reasons and, economically, for the supply of foods, such as sugar and spices. After the Industrial Revolution, colonies became more and more important for imports of agricultural and mineral raw materials. The conquerors built up public works in their colonies both to favour commerce and to improve the hygienic conditions of the population, not so much for humanitarian reasons (such reasons played only a collateral role), but in the interest of the growing number of their own public officials and businessmen. The death rate began to decline rapidly at the turn of the nineteenth century, owing to the rapid spread of hygienic and medical knowledge from the advanced countries. In underdeveloped countries, too, the birth rate started to decline, but with a longer lag; only after the 1960s did this decline become rapid in a growing number of underdeveloped countries. The second demographic explosion affecting the underdeveloped countries is now gradually slowing down, but it is still remarkable, and the absolute increase of their populations is still large; such an increase tends to aggravate poverty or makes it difficult for *per capita* incomes to rise.

The situation just sketched out is not much different from the one described by Malthus who, in developing his principle of population, was considering all countries, both advanced and primitive. Today in many underdeveloped countries the problems discussed by both Malthus and Ricardo have acquired new relevance.

Malthus' principle of population and Ricardo's diminishing returns in agriculture: the deadweight of 'routine'

Ricardo's view was that in agriculture the algebraic sum between diminishing returns and the productivity growth owing to technical progress was likely to be negative – in the sense that the increase of food production was likely to be slower than the increase of population. Ricardo took this view from Malthus. It has proved to be utterly wrong in the case of countries that were able to develop modern industry through innovations and to promote labour productivity in agriculture, introducing improvements in the methods of production largely based on capital goods produced by industry. In the countries that were unable to start a process of industrialization and where technical progress was largely absent in agriculture, we see Ricardo's tendency towards diminishing returns at work. More than that: in countries where peasants are struggling for survival they are unable to cope with soil erosion and, when they try to expand cultivable land or when they need wood for fuel, they reduce the forest area. This tends to upset the water regime, thus contributing to the process of desertification, which implies in turn that returns are not simply diminishing but tending to become negative. Such a trend is aggravated by the fact that peasants are uneducated and do not know even the simplest agricultural techniques – they often ignore even the use of natural fertilizers.

Here a digression is necessary. The above statement – that in several backward countries peasants ignore even the use of manure – may sound incredible. Yet, I saw as recently as 1960, at the border of Partinico, a little town not far from Palermo, manure accumulated not to be used but to be burned. At that time, the economy of that area was based on traditional agriculture; forty years later, the situation is radically different. At

much the same time I visited Stintino, a small village on the
sea coast in the North of Sardinia, a very lovely place. Until
the end of the nineteenth century the old inhabitants had been
shepherds in an island, Asinara, not far from there, but that
island had then been expropriated by the state, which built a
sanitary station for ships in quarantine and a penal colony.
The shepherds, brought to Stintino, where no pastures were
available, had to become fishermen; they learned, badly and
with great difficulty, how to fish, but they did not learn how
to swim, so that in rough seas some of their boats sank and not
a few of them drowned; in that village the number of widows
was above the norm. Clearly, men were deeply ignorant and
therefore did not have the mental agility to learn the art of
swimming. (I have since learned that the primitive inhabitants of the banks of the Mekong river, in Laos, also often know
how to fish but do not know to swim.) In Mexico, a population as relatively advanced as that of the Aztecs at the time
of the Spanish conquest had not yet invented the wheel,
except as a circular disk for describing the constellations and
interpreting the changes of the seasons in order to regulate
agricultural operations. Even the most simple and, for us,
most obvious arts require a minimum of culture. Otherwise
the dead weight of centuries-old traditions – of 'routine' – is
bound to dominate daily life.

Coming back to agriculture, we may presume that diminishing returns prevail when the rate of growth of people
working in the land is higher than the rate of increase of agricultural production whereas when this production is declining, there is a presumption of desertification. These,
however, are only presumptions since both phenomena can
be the consequence of other events, such as wars or ethnic
and social conflict. On the other hand, the statistical data for
seriously underdeveloped countries are not very reliable and
those concerning agriculture are particularly so, both for
reasons of organization and because the data on agricultural

output seldom include production for subsistence and the picking of wild fruits; on the other hand, food can also be obtained through hunting and fishing, in addition to imports. It is fitting to remember that several countries where we see signs of diminishing returns are, apart from their towns, not much beyond what Smith called the 'hunting stage'.

The hungry countries

The main reasons for the decline in agricultural output – originating negative and not only diminishing returns – are to be attributed to soil erosion and to deforestation, processes tending to upset the water regime, aggravating the consequences of droughts. This brings us to the problem of water availability, which is vital not only for agriculture but also for industry and for human beings – for hygienic conditions and for drinking: as a rule those countries are not only hungry but also thirsty. It is fitting to emphasize that the problem of water affects in various ways the whole of mankind, including the advanced countries. It is easy to predict that in the twenty-first century increasing resources will have to be devoted in all countries to the problem of water.

Table 6.2 presents two lists of countries. List I includes countries where there is evidence that diminishing returns in agriculture are probably at work, since the rate of increase of output is inferior to that of population. I have taken the rate of increase of population and not of the people employed in agriculture – more directly consistent with the views of Malthus and of Ricardo – since employment data are not available. List II includes countries where agricultural output is declining whereas population is increasing – a picture that is even more dramatic than that envisaged by Malthus and Ricardo. In table 6.2 I consider not only the difference between the two rates of change – output and population – but also the variations of food *per capita*.

Table 6.2 Agriculture and population, 1980–1993
(yearly rates of changes)

	Agricultural output 1980–93	Population 1980–93	Difference	Deforestation 1981–90	Food per capita 1979–93
I Agricultural output increasing more slowly than population					
Mozambique	1.4	1.7	−0.3	0.7	−2.1
Ethiopia	(2.0)	2.7	−0.7	0.3	−1.3
Burundi	2.7	2.9	−0.2	0.6	−0.3
Malawi	2.1	(2.9)	−0.8	1.4	−4.2
Madagascar	2.4	3.3	−0.9	0.8	−1.5
Kenya	2.6	3.3	−0.7	0.6	−0.4
Niger	(2.5)	3.3	−0.8	0.4	−1.8
Gambia	0.8	3.7	−2.9	0.8	−4.0
Zambia	2.5	3.4	−0.9	1.1	−0.3
Mongolia	2.0	2.6	−0.6	0.9	−2.5
Cent. Afr. Rep.	2.0	2.4	−0.4	0.4	−1.0
Mauritania	1.7	2.6	−0.9	0	−1.6
Zimbabwe	1.5	3.6	−2.1	0.7	−2.2
Myanmar	0.6	2.1	−1.5	..	−1.3
Philippines	1.2	2.3	−1.1	3.3	−1.3
Congo	2.6	2.9	−0.3	0.2	−1.5
Guatemala	1.8	2.9	−1.1	1.7	−0.5

Papua New Guinea	1.9	2.2	−0.3	0.3	−0.2
Dominican Rep.	0.4	2.2	−1.8	2.8	−1.8
Sierra Leone	1.2	2.5	−1.3	3.0	−1.2

II *Agricultural output declining, population increasing*

Rwanda	−0.2	2.9	−3.1	0.3	−2.5
Albania	−0.2	1.8	−2,0	0	−2.3
Nicaragua	−1.8	3.0	−4.8	1.9	−2.7
Côte d'Ivoire	−0.1	3.7	−3.8	1.0	−0.1
Lesotho	−0.5	2.9	−3.4	..	−2.2
Cameroon	−1.1	2.8	−3.9	0.6	−1.9
Bulgaria	−2.0	0	−2.0	..	−1.9

Note:

.. not available.

Sources: World Bank, *World Development Report*, 1994–6. The data of the last column (rate of change in food production *per capita*) are taken from the *World Development Report*, 1995, table 5; these largely coincide with those published in the *Human Development Report*, 1997.

Table 6.3 China and India, agricultural population, 1970–1997 (rates of change)

	Agricultural output			Population			Difference		
	1970–80	1980–90	1990–7	1970–80	1980–90	1990–7	1970–80	1980–90	1990–7
China	2.6	5.4	4.4	1.8	1.5	1.1	0.8	3.9	3.3
India	1.8	3.1	3.0	2.2	2.1	1.8	−0.4	1.0	1.2

We note that the majority of the countries considered (18 out of 27) belong to Africa South of the Sahara, four to Asia, three to America and two to Europe. Clearly, in several cases the poor performance depends on social upheavals and ethnic conflicts rather than on 'natural' circumstances.

For the most populous countries in the world (i.e. China, 1.2 billion and India, 1 billion) there is indirect evidence of diminishing returns in agriculture in the recent past, for example, in the 1950s and the 1960s – witness the recurrent famines that in certain years acquired mass dimensions. Today the situation of these two countries, together representing one-third of mankind, is much improved (table 6.3).

If, as seems likely, after the Second World War diminishing returns prevailed (though social unrest was also important), in more recent years the 'natural' tendency has been turned upside down by technical and organizational progress. The improvement, however, is also the result of the decline in the rate of increase of population that, in its turn, is to a certain extent the consequence of the policy of birth control, which in China has been very rigorous and has been much more successful than demographers deemed possible.

The natality and the fertility equations and child-producing poverty

On the basis of hypotheses put forward in different times by different demographers we can envisage that both the birth rate and the total fertility rate depend on the following variables; (1) gross national product (GNP) (Y), (2) infant mortality (IM), (3) the share of agricultural output over GNP (A) and (4) female illiteracy (FI) (see Livi Bacci, 1977).

Let us consider these four main explanatory variables one by one. (1) The higher the increase of income the greater the propensity of parents to preserve the improvement in the standard of living by restricting the number of children; at the same time, the higher the *per capita* income the higher the expenditure for raising and educating children. (2) The lower the infant mortality the lower the propensity of parents to have children, given the number of children that they intend to support beyond childhood. (3) The higher the share of agricultural output over GNP, the higher the propensity to have children; in fact, in poor countries, where agriculture is conducted with primitive methods, the peasants tend to have several children who can help them even at a very young age. (4) Women have to bear the main pain in the reproduction of mankind; so, when their cultural level increases they become more circumspect in their decision to have children; moreover, when they reach a certain degree of education, if they decide to work they often have to abjure having several children.

All demographic variables reflect the interaction between biological and social impulses, especially economic impulses. It is clear that both the birth rate (B) and the fertility rate (F) are influenced by variables that combine with different weights the underlying social or biological impulses. Therefore it is worthwhile to estimate two equations, one for the birth rate, the other for the total fertility rate, using the same explanatory variables, with reference to all the underdeveloped countries for which data are available, since we are interested in understanding the reasons for the demographic explosion and seeing what can be done to contract it in a relatively short time. Both the birth rate (B) and the fertility rate (F) are declining in almost all countries, so we will consider their speed of decline, which I take with a positive sign.

Also, owing to the availability of data, we consider: for the national product *per capita* the average rates of yearly change for the period 1985–94; for the birth rate and the fertility rate the differences between the years 1993 and 1970; for infant mortality the differences between the years 1994 and 1980; for agricultural production and female illiteracy the shares in

1994 and 1995.[1] No doubt, the four variables are to some extent interrelated, but apparently not to the point of making it necessary to abandon some of them (the Durbin–Watson (*DW*) test is acceptable in both equations):

$$B = 9.94 + 0.54\ \hat{Y} - 0.14\ IM - 0.11\ A - 0.08\ FI\ \bar{R}^2 = 0.65\ (B)$$
$$\quad\ 7.75\quad 3.53\qquad 4.60\qquad 2.43\qquad 3.25\ DW = 1.84$$

$$F = 2.38 + 0.11\ \hat{Y} - 0.02\ IM - 0.02\ A - 0.02\ FI\ \bar{R}^2 = 0.68\ (F)$$
$$\quad\ 7.86\quad 3.20\qquad 3.21\qquad 2.04\qquad 4.66\ DW = 1.94$$

Public authorities can influence the above variables in different ways and to different degrees. It is possible for them to exert direct influence on female illiteracy through a programme of education particularly addressed to women. The birth-rate equation (B) shows that in ten years a reduction of 1 percentage point in female illiteracy implies a diminution of 1 per cent in the birth rate. If we recognize that the death rate is as a rule near the minimum, it appears that a diminution of 1 per cent of the birth rate is by no means negligible and can make a substantial contribution to the reduction of the demographic explosion. The hungry countries of table 6.2 – where population growth outstrips that of agricultural output – have altogether about 500 million people – 8–9 per cent of mankind. Their yearly net increase of population is about 2.5 per cent (or 12–13 million), with a birth rate of 3.8 and a death rate of 1.3 per cent, near the minimum. A decrease of 10 percentage points in female illiteracy, which could be achieved in less than ten years, would reduce the birth rate from 3.8 to 2.8 per cent, implying a net increase of population of 7 instead of 12 million per year or 50 million

---

[1]   The data used for estimating equations (B) and (F) refer to 51 countries and are taken from World Bank, *World Development Report*, 1995 and 1996. I estimated (B) for the 18 countries of table 6.2 for which I found relevant data with equally satisfactory results; the values of the coefficients are as follows: 0.41 (*Y*), 0.08 (*IM*), 0.07 (*A*) and 0.14 (*FI*). $\bar{R}^2$ is 0.64 and *DW* is 2.34. This shows the 'robustness' of the estimates.

in ten years: a notable reduction. To prevent the birth of 50 million such suffering human beings is really an act of charity – let us speak, if we prefer, of solidarity or of far-sighted selfishness. The reduction of 50 million refers to the 'hungry countries' of table 6.2; we should emphasize that the reduction would be much greater if we considered several other backward countries. Let us not forget that, if it is true that the poor are concentrated in backward countries, especially in Africa, they represent a non-negligible share of the population of almost all countries: according to the World Bank, the poor, defined as persons obtaining a daily income of 1 US dollar or less, are about 1.2 billion – i.e. one-fifth of mankind. And it remains true that low education implies a relatively high birth rate in all countries.

A programme of women's education would have the additional advantage of not going directly against the prescriptions of certain religions, at least if we reject the damning hypothesis that the leaders of these religions might be hostile to such programmes in the conviction that women, once they had a higher level of education, would be more likely to use contraceptives. To dissipate such a suspicion leaders of these religions should demonstrate clearly that their intentions are different, by supporting vigorously (not simply through the worthy but fragmented activities of the missions) public programmes of women's education.

When poverty is associated with illiteracy, especially female illiteracy, the birth rate remains high and its decline very slow, thus making a considerable contribution to the world demographic explosion and to poverty: this is what we might call 'child-producing poverty'. Where mass education of women in principle meets with religious opposition, such opposition is strongest concerning propaganda for the use of contraceptives. Yet, such use can contribute not only to the reduction of the birth rate, but also to putting a brake on the diffusion of AIDS, that is ravaging certain countries, especially in Africa. Believers should remember that such prescriptions are not a matter of faith: they change in the course of time.

Naturally, the acceleration in the decline of the birth rate that can be obtained through a rise in the educational level of women is not the only benefit deriving from such a rise. For a proper appraisal of this as well as of other important benefits – concerning health, the education of children, poverty and a contribution to the process of growth – I refer to a publication of the World Bank (1993), where we find a survey of an important project for education in developing countries.

Africa and the problem of increasing poverty

Enzo Grilli, who has painstakingly gathered the data that allow us to form a general idea of long-term growth in developing countries, has emphasized that in such countries from 1870 to 1950 the rate of increase of real *per capita* income was very low (0.4–0.2 per cent per year), whereas it was of the order of 1.5 per cent per year in industrial countries (Grilli, 1994). In the last forty years the picture has become much more differentiated and more favourable to the developing countries considered as a whole (see table 6.4).

However, there are two striking contrasts between Asia and Africa South of the Sahara in the periods 1953–50 and 1973–90: in the first period the yearly rate of change of *per capita* income was negative in Asia (–0.4) and positive (1.4) in Africa South of the Sahara, in the second period it was 4.7 in Asia and – 1.0 in Africa South of the Sahara. The latter negative trend seems to have continued in recent years. In fact, the problems of increasing poverty, particularly in terms of food, are concentrated in Africa South of the Sahara, as table 6.2 shows. Almost all the non-African countries included in this table have been dislocated by social and political upheavals.

In his book on the economic prospects of developing countries Grilli shows (1999, table 4.5) that a sustained increase in *per capita* income started in various continents or

Table 6.4 *Developing countries, long-term growth,*
1953–1990 (per cent)

	1953–73	1973–90
Developing countries	2.6	2.9
Industrial countries	3.4	2.1

subcontinents in periods which were relatively restricted but significantly different: 1860–85 in Latin America, 1960–70 in Asia, 1890–1920 in North and South Africa, in 1950–70 in the rest of Africa; he makes the important caveat that not all the countries of the different continents have started a process of sustained growth.

These data emphasize the importance, for growth, of *territorial contiguity*: the forces of imitation, the circulation of ideas and of technical and commercial information as well as the facility of trade can explain the temporal clustering of those turning points. The contiguity effect is strengthened by the development of the means of transportation and communication, beginning with roads and railways.

The territorial contiguity and the other forces just mentioned enter in the explanation of the sequence of growth processes in the different Italian regions, from the North, to the Centre and – up to now, patchily – to the South.

We can express a cautious hope that some of the backward countries South of the Sahara, such as Mozambique and Angola, will enter into a spiral of development thanks to their contiguity with South Africa, a relatively dynamic country which is apparently overcoming recent epoch-making political changes without great traumas (an hypothesis that emerged in a conversation with Bruna Ingrao).

Here it is fitting to propose a particular reflection. Argentina was one of the first countries in Latin America to start a process of growth – the indicative date is 1860. In 1913 the *per capita* income of Argentina was estimated to be 50 per cent higher than that of Italy; today it is less than one-half – since 1913 the *per capita* income of both countries has increased, but that of Argentina much less than that of Italy. I am inclined to attribute the poor long-run performance of Argentina to two particular factors. First, Argentina concentrated its economy on a very limited number of commodities – particularly cereals and meat – which in the course of time had mostly negative vicissitudes in international markets. Second, the development of manufactures was not only late but also vitiated by tariff protection and the lack of efforts to promote investment in research. In any case, the case of Argentina shows that reaching a relatively high level of *per capita* income cannot be seen as a permanent achievement.

Grilli (1999, ch. V) analyses at length the inverse correlation between economic growth and poverty. This correlation is clear, but it is neither strict nor mechanically determined: given the rate of economic growth, the share of the poor can be more or less reduced depending on redistributional policies which, in their turn, depend on the cultural and political situation of each country.

The problem of rooting out poverty is of course worldwide, but is acute in Africa South of the Sahara precisely because the prospects for an increase of *per capita* income are gloomy in most of these countries. The reasons, listed in a 1989 report of the World Bank, are various – the list looks like that of Job's misfortunes:

- Deterioration in the terms of trade, caused first of all by falling prices – until recently, of oil and of several raw materials
- High population pressure
- Desertification and deforestation
- Heavy foreign debt
- Awful health conditions (AIDS, tuberculosis, malaria – especially cerebral malaria – are three great killers)
- Ethnic conflicts and political instability, which make it difficult to begin any reform.

To be sure, such misfortunes, which to some extent are inter-related, do not appear to be evenly distributed and some of the countries show a record that is not particularly bad. Moreover, certain more recent changes can help, such as the recovery in the price of oil and the lessening of social and political conflicts. But the overall picture remains dark.

The changing inequality in income distribution during the process of development

The reduction of poverty depends to a non-negligible extent on economic policy – particularly fiscal transfers from the rich to the poor and easy and cheap loans to the poor to help them to start very small economic activities. Clearly, economic policy and especially fiscal policy can be more and more effective as the development process goes on. Here the question of the behaviour of income inequality in the different phases of the process becomes relevant. This question was originally studied by Simon Kuznets (1965), who pointed out that the degree of inequality in a first phase of development increases and subsequently tends to decrease – that is, it takes the form of a parabola with upward concavity, having the shape of an inverted U. However, neither Kuznets nor the economists who followed him have proposed a fully-fledged explanation of such behaviour and a few economists have even put it in question. Yet, in my view that behaviour as a rule is real, and its explanation is not very difficult to find.

If it is true that development is driven by all sorts of innovations – technological and organizational – and if it is true that for this reason it is, by necessity, an unbalanced process, as Schumpeter long ago emphasized, then it does not and cannot affect all activities simultaneously and with the same intensity. Even the simple but important model developed by Arthur Lewis, in which a modern sector appears in a primitive economy, implies a sharp increase in income inequality in its first phase. The activities giving rise to such a sector often originate a process of growth: this process is not spread evenly over the territory of the country, but is located in particular areas. The innovating activities distribute incomes – profits and wages – which are higher than those distributed by the other activities, which are affected only indirectly and with various time lags. Development tends to be cumulative, but it is still an unbalanced process. Yet, as long as the innovating activities represent a minority – though a particularly dynamic minority – in the economy and as long as they are territorially concentrated in relatively restricted areas, the inequality in income distribution tends to increase. When the social weight of innovating activities exceeds a critical threshold and spreads throughout the territory, then the process still remains unbalanced, but the inequality in income distribution tends to decrease.

The behaviour of the index of inequality is far from being uniform in different countries, since it depends on the types of innovating activities, on the velocity of their expansion and on their localization as well as on the policy adopted. This means that that behaviour is bound to be very uneven. In fact, in the cross-section analysis presented in my earlier book on underdevelopment (Sylos Labini, 1983a, pp. 111, 224), in a diagram showing the relation between *per capita* income and degree of inequality, the points relating to the various countries at different levels of development are placed, not on a parabola, but in an area whose boundaries are given by two parabolas, one above the other, indicating the indeterminateness of the Kuznets curve, which justifies the economists who do not recognize the very existence of that curve – perhaps it would be preferable to speak of a 'Kuznets belt'.

The policy aimed at fighting poverty is more likely to be successful the higher the *per capita* income of the country considered. A preliminary indication of the success of such a policy can be given by the extent of the downward shift in two different periods of the point referring to the country in the Kuznets belt.

7

Dependent workers, employment and unemployment

Traditional communities and the labour market: wage employment and independent workers

If we recognize that economics as a science is historically and thus also geographically conditioned, since at a given time different societies experience different stages of development, then we have to use labels and definitions of economists very carefully. This is particularly true in the case of labourers and of labour incomes. At the same time, we have to be well aware that societies are far from being homogeneous. Thus, advanced societies have sectors that are both poor and underdeveloped, from the standpoint of methods of production as well as of ways of life. On the other hand, in underdeveloped countries we find sectors that are relatively advanced – sometimes these sectors have been promoted by foreign companies in their own interest.

In this context, the label 'self-employed' or 'independent workers' means different things in the two categories of country. In low-income countries 'independent workers' often mean active members of traditional communities, such as those constituting villages. In such areas, the labour market simply does not exist, although as a rule a kind of product market does exist: members of these communities bring part of the goods that they produce to the small markets of the towns. In the same countries, outside the village communities we find 'independent workers' with features somewhat similar to those of the members of cooperatives or to the 'self-employed' of advanced countries. In general, in underdeveloped countries 'independent workers' represent the great majority of the labour force – in 1994, they comprised 83 per cent, whereas they were 43 per cent in middle-income countries and only 16 per cent in advanced countries (World Bank, *World Development Report*, 1995, p. 72). 'Dependent workers' represent the complements to 100 of these shares. Yet, it would be improper to treat dependent workers and wage workers as equivalent, as most economists do, since wage employment needs to be distinguished from salary employment if we admit that the factors of wage change do not coincide with those of salary change. In addition, the factors concerning salary change in the private sector differ from those concerning salary change in the public sector. Finally, in both advanced and underdeveloped countries the treatment of dependent workers employed in relatively large firms differs radically from that of dependent workers employed in small or very small firms. Another clear distinction is between workers inside and outside agriculture.

According to Marx, the trend towards wage earning – the proletariat – was increasing all over the world, the advanced countries anticipating the evolution of all the other countries. This has not been so. In the advanced countries the number of wage earners, after a period of expansion, ceased to rise – the maximum was 50–60 per cent of the active population – whereas the number of salary earners increased in both absolute and relative terms; moreover, independent workers have not declined, and in certain countries have even increased. Thus the famous forecast, to be found in Marx's *Communist Manifesto* (Marx and Engels, 1959 [1848]), according to which the proletariat was to become the overwhelming majority of the population, has proved to be totally wrong. Looking at the world as a whole, in many countries wage earners represent a minority of the population and, considering the systematically increasing weight of salary earners and the persistence of independent workers, there is no sign that they will follow the evolution predicted by Marx. The question is also politically important, since Marx's prediction was intended to justify, so to speak, the dictatorship of the proletariat, which would have been painful for the exploiters, who were doomed to become a tiny share of the population. The irony of history was that the catastrophic Bolshevik Revolution took place in a country where the 'proletariat' in the Marxian sense had a negligible weight.[1]

The informal sector, child labour and women workers

In both the underdeveloped and the advanced economies there is an informal sector, where we find very small firms and irregular workers. The definition of the 'informal sector' is not easy: often the units operating there are outside or even against the law; in fact, they are tolerated by the authorities *faute de mieux*, to favour employment, even of a precarious type. Units operating in the informal sector do not pay taxes and welfare contributions and do not comply with the regulations for the safety of workers. Often they employ children, paying their parents very low wages; child labour is widespread in underdeveloped Asian countries and is frequent in African countries. The same is true for women workers, who in all countries are as a rule paid less than males; in the informal sector, the gap becomes particularly pronounced.

In more recent times the appearance of an informal sector has often been the consequence of laws that have tended to

---

[1] Even in the midst of tragedy we can find persons endowed with courage and with a strong sense of humour; a member of the Russian Communist Party was so bold as to make the following remark in the presence of Lenin, at the 1922 XI Party Congress in Moscow: 'Yesterday Vladimir Ilyich [Lenin] declared that the proletariat as a class and in the Marxian sense did not exist [in Russia]. Let me congratulate you for exercising a dictatorship in the name of a class that does not exist' (Various authors, *Le livre noir du communisme*, 1997, p. 808).

give guarantees to those working in official firms. To some extent this is true also for underdeveloped countries, where modern firms (often representing a small minority) are regulated in ways similar to that operating in developed countries. Certain international agreements to this effect have in fact been signed not only by the governments of the advanced but also by many governments of the underdeveloped countries. But it is one thing to approve a law, another to apply it in practice.

However, in underdeveloped countries, and especially in the poorest of them, the very meaning of the 'informal sector' is different from that applicable to industrial countries. In underdeveloped countries the guarantees for all workers, including those of the formal sector, are much weaker than in industrial countries and the distinction itself between the two sectors is uncertain. Since for many people to work in the informal sector is the only way to survive, the authorities are compelled to tolerate a 'black economy'. In spite of this, a policy to help the workers of the informal sector to enter the formal one is to be recommended even in underdeveloped countries; such a policy should be gradual and carefully implemented. The question becomes extremely difficult in the case of the exploitation of child labour, very common in underdeveloped countries, but not unknown (though having different features) in industrial countries. The fundamental criterion should be of not limiting oneself to a blanket prohibition – often the labouring children constitute a means of survival for their parents – but of introducing, perhaps with some international aid, workable alternatives. One of these is to create incentives for sending the children to school – for instance, supplying free food. Another is to create favourable conditions in their search for regular employment to parents with small children, especially to mothers, encouraging the spread of part-time jobs.

From empirical enquiries promoted by the World Bank (see the *World Development Report*, 1995) two things emerge clearly: (1) the informal sector is the larger the lower is the degree of development of the country and (2) in the informal sector not only child labour but also working women are relatively more numerous than in the formal sector, in both underdeveloped and advanced countries. Fragmentary indications show that the size of the informal sector tends to decrease in the ascending phases and to increase in the descending phases of the business cycle.

Since units operating in the informal economy do not pay taxes and welfare contributions, they are in a position to bring unfair competition to firms in the formal economy that produce similar goods. Moreover, they can fire workers without safeguards even in countries in which legal guarantees are relatively strict. Firms in the informal sector have, however, several disadvantages: they cannot grow beyond certain limits, otherwise they inevitably enter the area that lies within the reach of public authorities; they find it very difficult to introduce innovations and they find it even more difficult to export – to this end they have to resort to intermediaries operating in the official economy, thus losing a share of their profits. On the other hand, they face serious problems if their workers are hit by industrial accidents. All in all, the informal units can find it expedient to emerge and enter the formal economy; policies directed to this end can therefore, through various types of incentives, be successful, especially in the case of units that are near a regular status and can, therefore, relatively easily be induced to make the shift. Other units, however, are so inefficient that even strong incentives can have little effect.

We have also to be aware that a good proportion of the people working in the informal economy appear as 'unemployed' in the official statistics. From one point of view this could be interpreted in a relatively optimistic manner: 'you see', it has been said in Italy with reference to the South, where today (1999) the official figure of unemployment is more than 22 per cent, 'the devil is not so bad as it looks'.

However, this interpretation is to be rejected, because employment in the informal economy, though better than nothing, is, for the reasons just mentioned, to be viewed as a pathological phenomenon – we can speak of 'pathological employment'.

Migrations and the labour market in advanced countries

In advanced countries the informal sector includes not only informal firms and a number of independent workers, but also people working irregularly and immigrants from poor countries, who often work seasonally in rural firms.

After the Second World War, international migrations, that had shrunk to low levels after 1918, due also to the Great Depression, showed a rapid increase – however, with a great variety of situations, according to countries and to periods. As Graziella Caselli has pointed out, we must distinguish three periods: 1950–73 (sustained economic growth in advanced countries), 1973–90 (slow economic growth) and 1990 onwards: after the crumbling of the Berlin Wall, migrations from Eastern Europe and from the countries of the Former Soviet Union (FSU) toward Western Europe and North America became important (Caselli, 1994).

Migrations that were facilitated by progress in the means of transportation received the main impulse from the poverty of certain underdeveloped countries that, owing to the demographic pressures, is stable or even increasing, in sharp contrast with the increasing welfare of advanced countries. However, in certain countries and in certain periods political and ethnic conflicts have been no less important. Nor should we underrate the stimulus to migration from poor to rich countries originated by the latter's low and even decreasing birth rate.

In the labour market of advanced countries persons coming from poor countries are often ready to accept jobs refused by natives and, when there are vacancies in unskilled jobs even in the presence of widespread unemployment, immigrants fill the gap. These problems are worth analysing not only for the sake of a better understanding of migratory flows, but also to make clear the serious limitations of the models of the labour market developed by mainstream economists, based on three main assumptions: (1) a homogeneous labour force, (2) unchanged technologies and (3) a closed national market. Migrations, the dynamic substitution of machinery for labour and the changes in the composition of exports and of imports depending on changes in the international division of labour are thus neglected.

Let us systematically reconsider the analysis that starts with the dichotomy in the labour market between skilled and unskilled workers. If in an advanced country the wages of unskilled workers increase, managers hire people coming from underdeveloped countries to put a halt to the increase in those wages. Alternatively, managers import those intermediate products highly intensive in the use of unskilled labour that cost less than similar goods produced at home. Still another alternative is to introduce labour-substituting machinery – the choice will be made after a cost comparison of the different alternatives. If the process goes on, and these alternatives are not sufficient, then an increasing amount of finished goods will be imported from underdeveloped countries, whereas those produced at home will be made more and more by independent workers enjoying special advantages, or by firms capable of differentiating their products. Finally, firms in the advanced country in question will transfer abroad, where wages are lower, all the operations they can, or even whole factories. The spectrum of possibilities, then, is large.

Three statements can be made regarding migrations from developing to developed countries, such as those currently taking place:

- First, if it is true that the great majority of immigrants from developing countries are unskilled workers, it is also true that a small share of them consists of skilled or highly skilled workers, including doctors, scientists and educators, which represents a great loss for the sending countries.
- Second, if highly skilled workers who emigrate from a developing country to an advanced country go back to their mother country when conditions at home improve they can bring with them very valuable experience. The case often mentioned is that of Indian returnees from Silicon Valley in the United States, who have strongly contributed to the growth of the software industry in India. The Indians in Silicon Valley and in other parts of the world who became experts in IT are apparently so numerous that the German government is considering calling no less than 30,000 Indian experts to Germany. The idea is to be condemned, since it is better that those Indians remain in their mother country. Given the great need of IT experts – in firms, in public administration, in schools, universities and research institutions – the whole European Union should organize an Institute for a rapid formation of IT experts to be employed in Europe. Not only the number, but also the skill of such experts can improve owing to the variety of specializations in the different countries.
- Third, migrations can be advantageous for both the sending and the receiving countries, if they are adequately managed. This is particularly true for Europe, which is facing immigration from countries of very different cultural and economic backgrounds. In such a situation a common European policy needs to be worked out and applied much more systematically than it is the case at present. Two approaches are worth studying: temporary programmes and schemes of

self-management by immigrants; the *World Bank Report*, 1995 is a good basis on which to reflect on such programmes.

Employment and unemployment in advanced countries.

Migrations from developing towards developed countries imply variations in the labour force, in employment and unemployment of both countries; let us first consider the latter.

To interpret the behaviour of employment in developed countries we may use the productivity equation presented in chapter 3 (p. 68). In a first approximation, we consider only wage workers; Keynes' simple employment equation implyed proportionality between the level of income and that of employment, since Keynes assumed techniques as given. We remain with the same logic if from levels we move to rates of change, and write $\hat{Y} = \hat{N}$, where Y is income, N is wage employment and the circumflex (^) indicates a yearly rate of change. If we admit that techniques change, then we have

$$\hat{Y} = \hat{N} + \hat{\pi} \quad \text{or} \quad \hat{N} = \hat{Y} - \hat{\pi}$$

where π is labour productivity. Recalling the productivity equation, we can write, putting

$$b' = 1 - b$$

the following equation

$$\hat{N} = -a + b'\hat{Y} - c\,(\hat{W} - \hat{P}_{ma})_{-m} + dI_{-n} - e\,(\hat{L} - \hat{P}) \tag{7.1}$$

This is the employment equation. In the productivity equation, $b\hat{Y}$ indicates the Smith effect, that pushes up productivity. Given $1 > b > 0$, then $b' = 1 - b$ is positive and $b'\hat{Y}$ indicates the Keynes effect, that pushes up employment ($Y = C + I$: consumption and investment feed effective demand). Assuming that the labour force does not change, then the variations of employment correspond, with the opposite sign, to those of unemployment, conceived in the strict sense – that is, workers who have lost or have abandoned their job. To pass to total unemployment, UN, which includes people in search of a first job, we have to admit that the labour force is not constant, allowing for immigration, the natural increase of population and for persons entering into (or leaving) the labour market; we must then also include among the arguments the rate of change of the labour force, FL. Granting that unemployment is equal to the difference between the labour force and employment ($UN = FL - N$), then the rate of change in unemployment is

$$U\hat{N} = a + a'\hat{FL} - b'\hat{Y} + c\,(\hat{W} - \hat{P}_{ma}) - dI - e\,(\hat{L} - \hat{P}) \qquad (7.2)$$

I have tested the above equations for several countries and several periods: they explain both employment and unemployment reasonably well (Sylos Labini, 1990).[2] Within the year-by-year variations of productivity that govern the variations of employment and unemployment, we find minor innovations stimulated by the Smith and the Ricardo effects; in turn, these minor innovations and adaptations depend on major innovations and major inventions, which cannot be explained directly by economic factors.

The main impulses determining the variations of unemployment thus come from income, investment and labour productivity. In such an analysis, however, a particular factor

---

[2] The productivity equation, from which I have derived the employment and unemployment equations, explains very well not only the productivity slowdown that occurred in American industry in the 1980s (ch. 3, p. 69), but also the productivity rise that has occurred in recent years. The average yearly rates of change of productivity, of the Smith effect and of the Ricardo effect in the two periods are as follows:

	1977–82	1991–8
Productivity ($\hat{\pi}$)	0.1	1.6
Smith effect ($\hat{Y}$)	0.6	4.4
Ricardo effect ($\hat{W} - \hat{P}_{ma}$)	0.2	4.1

is missing that many economists today consider the most important of all, that is, flexibility in the labour market – flexibility in wages, in the duration of contracts and of the working week and in the conditions for firing redundant workers. The evidence put forward to support this thesis is generally drawn from comparisons between the United States and the countries of continental Europe. In the former, where flexibility in the labour market is judged to be high, the increase of employment in the last twenty or thirty years has been very large – 20 million from 1980 to 1998. Today in the United States the unemployment rate is near the frictional level, that in our time can be estimated at around 5 per cent. In continental Europe, instead, employment has increased slowly and in the 1990s unemployment also increasing being now at around 10 per cent, with peaks, in certain areas, of more than 40 per cent.

There is no doubt that flexibility has strongly contributed to these contrasted performances. Yet, in the 1950s and 1960s, when flexibility in Europe was even lower than today, the rate of unemployment was not far from the frictional level. How can we explain this paradox?

The explanation is probably that when output and investment are increasing at a sustained rate, then unemployment can be low even if the degree of flexibility is low – and, in particular, if the possibility for managers of firing redundant workers is restricted: in a rapidly expanding economy the main problem is to hire, not to fire. In fact, until the first oil shock of 1973 the growth rate of industrial countries was relatively high – on average, more than 4 per cent per year (Maddison, 1998). After 1973, however, that rate about halved and flexibility began to become a problem, in particular flexibility concerning the liberty of firing. To reduce the gravity of this problem trade unions could, for instance, introduce a clause graduating wages and severance pay in relation to the liberty of firing in labour contracts.

By taking the ratio between investment and income (I/Y) as

a synthetic expression of the impulses governing the variations of unemployment (Y, I and labour productivity, that
affects both Y and I), one can estimate that this ratio should
be 4 or 5 points higher in countries with low flexibility, such
as those of continental Europe, than in countries with high
flexibility, such as Great Britain and the United States. To
take a numerical example: in the countries of continental
Europe the ratio I/Y should be 20 per cent instead of 15 per
cent to obtain an unemployment of 5 or 6 per cent (Sylos
Labini, S., 1997). And since in the new international scenario
it is very unlikely that industrial countries will succeed in
reaching rates of growth and I/Y ratios similar to those of the
1950s and 1960s, then in continental Europe it is necessary
to exert great efforts to raise significantly the degree of flexibility in labour markets.

The link between flexibility and the interplay of the
impulses just mentioned (Y and I) is given by *wage changes*.
However, the flexibility of wages should not be considered in
isolation – or, worse still, in a static framework – but in relation to other variables. Thus, if the possibility of firing
workers is restricted, then, *ceteris paribus*, the downward
flexibility of wages will be low, whereas, by the same token,
the upward flexibility will be high. More than that: in a
country where the possibility of firing is restricted, then managers, when the demand for their products is rising, will tend
to expand output, not so much by hiring additional workers
but, whenever possible, by introducing new machines. The
consequence is that in such a country productivity will –
again, *ceteris paribus* – increase more quickly than in a
country where it is easier to fire workers. In other words,
given the increase in demand, in the former country the
increase of output will be carried out mainly by means of a
productivity increase and, only secondarily, by increasing
employment. In a country where firing is easy, the two contributions are similar.

The figures in table 7.1 referring to Italy and to the United

Table 7.1 *Change in income, employment and productivity, Italy and the United States, 1970–1995*

	$\hat{Y}$	$\hat{N}$	$\hat{\pi}$
Italy	2.7	0.5	2.2
United States	2.8	1.2	1.6

States as representatives of the two types of country, illustrate this point: in the period 1970–95 in Italy 20 per cent of the increase of income could be attributed to the increase of employment and 80 per cent to the increase of productivity, whereas in the United States the corresponding figures were 43 and 57 per cent. In the relevant period in the two countries the yearly rates of change in income, employment and productivity are as in table 7.1 (Sylos Labini, 1999).

However, the better performance of employment in the United States is not to be attributed principally to the higher degree of flexibility in the labour market. Flexibility in its various forms is a favourable condition, but it is not and cannot be an impulse. The main impulse is given by investment that, via demand, immediately affects income and employment (the Keynes effect): only after a delay does it influence productivity, whose increase, taken in itself, depresses the level of employment, which does not decline if a fresh increase in investment occurs. Given the increases in investment and in income, the positive effect on employment will be the greater the higher the degree of flexibility: this is another way of considering the relation, discussed above, between the ratio I/Y and employment. A high flexibility can favour the actual expansion of output.

If we consider the United States, and concentrate our attention on investment in more recent years, we can list a series of factors facilitating the expansion of investment. First, private investment, which has been supported by the intelligent credit policy adopted by the Federal Reserve System – its

President aims at supporting growth minimising the inflationary pressures, but, correctly, considers the behaviour of
unemployment and of wages as well as that of raw materials
and energy prices much more relevant that variations in the
money supply (Greenspan, 2000). Second, public investment,
and particularly its composition – expenditure for research,
for military and civilian purposes – is relevant even now.
Moreover, there are the effects of the large expenditure of this
type made in the past: the fallout of the innovations promoted
by such expenditure on the private sector is still important.
Third, the behaviour of raw materials and energy prices, that
until the late 1990s was declining: this kept inflation low, thus
favouring a liberal credit policy. Fourth, although the credit
policy has been liberal, interest rates in the United States are,
on average, 2 points higher than in Europe, with a consequent
significant flow of capital toward that country. Finally, the
dollar is a reserve currency, and this has allowed a trade
deficit that no other countries could afford.

If it is true that low flexibility encourages productivity
growth, then an increase of this magnitude may depress such
growth and this in the long run has negative consequences on
international competitiveness; I believe that the increasing
US trade deficit to some extent depends on the deterioration
of the competitiveness in several traditional areas of production. Moreover, in years of slow development or of stagnation, high flexibility brings with it declining real wages, with
negative effects on the demand for consumption goods. The
problem is thus to find an optimum degree of flexibility,
which is not the maximum degree possible.

As for the relations between the rates of change in income
and in employment, we have to take into account the fact that
such relations have to be considered in the wider context
shown in (7.1), in which the degree of flexibility in the labour
market is reflected mainly in the behaviour of wages. In any
case, those relations in developing countries are as a rule different from those that can be observed in industrial countries:

in general, it is possible to state that 'the employment-generation capacity of output growth appears to be considerably higher in developing than in industrial countries' (Grilli and Zanalda, 1999, p. 5). However, in a previous stage these countries showed a higher employment elasticity with respect to income not very different from that observable today in developing countries: 0.5; today in industrial countries that value has fallen to 0.2 (such values are averages concerning several countries and several years) (Grilli and Zanalda, 1999, p. 9). Presumably these differences are to be attributed first of all to the behaviour of real wages, that condition the variations in productivity and, conversely, those of employment.

Up to now I have considered dependent workers – wage and salary earners. The situation is different for the self-employed, be they working individually or with family aids, which is rather common in agriculture and handicraft. The self-employed can become unemployed if the goods they produce enter into competition with goods produced by firms at decreasing costs and prices. As I hinted in chapter 5 (p. 103), the self-employed enjoy certain advantages that allow them, up to a point, to resist the competition of firms located in their own countries or in underdeveloped countries, where wages are much lower. In fact, the self-employed are in a better position to modify the type or the design of the goods they produce and to find new niches in internal or international markets; they can also better modulate the supply of effort to the changes in demand. But when, in spite of such protection, the self-employed are beaten in competition, then they have to abandon their business. If they have acquired some useful skill, they can shift into firms and become dependent workers. This shift can occur either within one of the three major sectors (agriculture, industry, services) or into a different sector – the self-employed in agriculture often become dependent workers in industry.

In such an incessant turmoil, in the final analysis originated by all sorts of innovations, the whole educational system, including formation of workers, must be flexible enough to allow young people to adapt themselves when they change their jobs. Moreover, it should be directed not only towards young but also towards old people. In fact, with the rise in life expectancy and the systematic improvement in health conditions, the number of old people capable of being active members of society is rapidly increasing in advanced countries. Recognizing that for most people the ideal is not '*il dolce far niente*' (the sweetness of doing nothing), as idleness means boredom, but to work with satisfaction, then a number of old people in good health should be put in a position to perform some useful activity – assistance to sick people, teaching foreign languages, assistance to children, guides to museums or archaeological sites, etc.

Unemployment in Europe

Today the average rate of unemployment in Europe (10 per cent) is pathologically high; in certain regions the figure is considerably higher – it is more than 20 per cent in the South of Italy, for example. It is true that a good part of such figures does not represent unemployed people, but people working irregularly or in the informal sector. These people, however, cannot be considered as economically advantageously employed: they represent a social problem.

In a 'Manifesto' to combat unemployment in Europe, promoted by Franco Modigliani, in which I collaborated (Modigliani *et al.*, 1998), we argued that the European Union had to work out a strategy based on an expansion of both private and public investment and a marked increase in flexibility in labour markets, stimulating especially the spread of part-time jobs. We warned, however, that an increase of flexibility taken by itself could not reduce unemployment, while it could strengthen the positive effects on employment of an increase in investment.

As for private investment, we maintained that the European Central Bank (ECB) should adopt an appropriate monetary policy, similar to that followed in recent years in the United States by the Federal Reserve System, which favoured growth without being paralysed by a fear of inflation, that in our time had come fundamentally from cost pressures and from certain movements in exchange rates.

As for public investment, the European strategy should promote infrastructures of two types: (1) large infrastructures, especially in the field of telecommunications, affecting all the countries of the Union, and (2) local infrastructures, especially in underdeveloped regions of Europe to accelerate the growth of industrial districts, including research organizations to diffuse innovations.

A third recommendation in our strategy was to transform, whenever possible, subsidies or social transfers to the unemployed into incentives to production – for instance, by giving very cheap loans to the unemployed to start new small businesses. A similar criterion is to be recommended in redistributional policies aimed at alleviating poverty.

Employment and unemployment in underdeveloped countries

Employment in underdeveloped countries in the low-income category is a problematic concept. The members of village communities are in a sense self-employed, though the differences from the self-employed of advanced countries are overwhelming. They can hardly become unemployed, even if some of them, from the point of view of production, are or become redundant. In certain groups, problems of unemployment of a special type can arise.

Let us consider two cases: that of the Indian artisans at the beginning of the nineteenth century, producing textiles; and that of the rural families in the South of Italy after Unification, producing non-agricultural goods, again, very simple textiles. The case of the Indian artisans is particularly interesting. In the first stage of English industrialization, which affected primarily the cotton industry, Indian hand-made textile products created vigorous competition to English products, since the Indian artisans could live on extremely modest incomes. England, then, introduced duties to protect home products. In the course of time, however, the productivity of English workers increased so much, thanks to the introduction of machines of increasing efficiency, that English firms were in a position to move to the counterattack: the duties were removed, England gradually adopted a free trade policy and her producers were able to export textiles to India, where the local artisans were beaten in competition by imports. According to the picturesque (and doubtful) description given by Marx, many of the Indian weavers, 'because of English machines', starved and 'their bones . . . had to "bleach in the sun"' (quoted by Schumpeter, 1954, p. 685). Owing to technical progress occurring in England, those Indian artisans lost their jobs and, according to Marx, even their lives.

The second case is that of textiles produced by women more than a century ago in rural families in the South of Italy, with the help of very simple instruments – a type of production similar, though not identical, to that of the so-called 'cottage industry' in Great Britain in the eighteenth century. These women were producing textiles for the use of their own families or in exchange for goods produced by other rural families, or for sale. The number of such women, included in the industrial censuses, was relatively high in 1881 – more than 1 million; it fell to less than half a million in 1901 (SVIMEZ, 1961, p. 51). This fall was apparently largely caused by the competition from machine-made goods, mostly produced in the North of Italy, which at that time was entering into the stage of modern industrialization. The number of women working in 'industry' in the South of Italy subsequently continued to fall.

In developed countries, innovating activities determine the transformation or the decline of traditional activities. This process takes time and it gives rise to an algebraic sum that in certain periods is positive, in others negative: the aggregate employment rises if demand increases more rapidly than productivity. When innovating activities have destructive effects in other countries, then in such countries the algebraic sum tends to be negative, unless some of the local activities expand and so offset the negative effects coming from abroad.

When the algebraic sum is the result of internal impulses, governments can try to protect the imperilled traditional activities. Thus, after the Second World War the Indian government introduced special taxes on modern textile firms to lessen their competitive pressure on traditional handicrafts which since time immemorial had undergone deep adaptation and were still important from the point of view of employment. In general, if protective measures are such as to help traditional units to become more and more efficient, then those measures can be approved; otherwise, they soon become harmful.

Again, in India after the Second World War special taxes were imposed on farms that were mechanizing their productive operations, thus increasing unemployment among landless peasants. This type of measures can also be justified for only limited periods.

In underdeveloped countries urbanization can also be a source of unemployment: very poor people living in rural areas go to the towns hoping to find a job. They seldom find a regular job, at least at first; thus, they remain unemployed or find precarious low-income jobs. The distinction between unemployment, on the one side, and precarious employment, underemployment, pathological and irregular employment, on the other, is very subtle indeed: these concepts largely overlap, although do not fully coincide (Sylos Labini, 1964).

A peculiar and important type of unemployment is one

that appeared in those centrally planned economies that in recent years dismantled a sizable part of their central and local administrations and promoted the privatization of public enterprises. This occurred, with different intensities, in all the countries of the Soviet Bloc and in China. It seems that in Russia the process of change has taken on chaotic features; many public employees have not had their salaries for months, though formally they have not lost their jobs. In China in recent years this type of unemployment assumed less chaotic features, but more massive dimensions.

In underdeveloped countries, no less than in industrial economies, the innovations directly or indirectly determining a reduction in labour input can generate unemployment if aggregate demand does not increase fast enough. But innovations consisting in the production of new goods tend to increase employment, provided that the negative effects on similar production competing with the new goods are not quickly felt. In agriculture, if the mechanization of productive operations creates unemployment, irrigation systems, on the contrary, can have decidedly positive effects on employment and need to be stimulated on both large- and small-scale farms. The same applies to innovations in biotechnologies, such as those produced in the laboratories of the Rockefeller Foundation in Mexico City, concerning new varieties of wheat and corn and starting, especially in India, the well known 'Green Revolution'. True, not all the experts express a positive judgement on this Revolution: some are critical, owing to the unbalances created in Indian agriculture as a whole. To be sure, the introduction of an innovation of such magnitude should be carefully managed, by carrying out a preliminary study of the different types of land and a plan to adequately inform and assist the peasants. Probably such preparation was insufficient in India, although some unbalance is in any case inevitable. Yet, we do well to reflect on the lessons that we can draw from such an experience for future action.

8

Organizational and institutional innovations

Reforms to create a growth-oriented market

Understanding the growth process brings us to how to accelerate it. Measures of economic policy can have more than ephemeral success only if they are based on appropriate organizational and institutional innovations. I shall present in this chapter some reflections on a strategy of reforms that can lead to fostering sustainable economic growth. If we consider the distinction among low-, middle- and high-income countries, we have to be well aware that such a partition, that appears to be quantitative, presupposes a great variety of routes and thus a great variety of problems. In keeping with the Smithian approach adopted here, each country requires a preliminary study of the main lines of its historical evolution: quantities, considered in isolation, are misleading.

Economic growth cannot be seen as an unmixed blessing. In its course, it destroys many traditional values and creates deep changes in ways of life and in systems of ideas: the uninterrupted process of adaptation cannot go on without suffering. It is then understandable that certain regimes place restraints on the growth process, mainly for ethical and religious reasons. And yet, after certain countries have entered into a process of growth, other countries have been compelled to follow, either to preserve or to regain their independence or to obtain advantages similar to those that the pioneer countries obtained in terms of improved living conditions.

Growth represents a socially fundamental goal as long as the *per capita* income of the majority of the population falls short of a critical level, where the people are in a position to satisfy their basic needs, including those concerning health, and to obtain a certain amount of comfort. Beyond that level, economic growth becomes less and less important and consumerism tends to spread, assuming pathological features: tourism expands, which can be judged positively, but the flow of frivolous or even harmful goods swells. With the increase of *per capita* income the length of labour time declines, leisure increases and the quality of labour – that is, the satisfaction that can be obtained in working – and the correspondence between studies undergone and the type of job available, acquires increasing relevance.

Growth is thus still an important goal for mankind, especially for backward countries. And if the strategies to follow are bound to be different, depending on the level and distribution of income, the basic mechanism to be adopted or improved is the market. In fact, of the various experiments carried out by mankind, it appears that this mechanism is the most suited to pursue economic growth. If it is true that the market is not a vacuum, but an institutional framework, then to initiate or to accelerate a growth process the first necessity is to determine what are the legal reforms that can create a growth-oriented market.

In discussing a strategy of any kind of reform we do well to recognize that the most fruitful and most revolutionary changes in social life are those introduced gradually and made compatible as far as possible with tradition, since changes of this kind can minimize the resistance of the people and maximize their propensity to learn the most rational means to promote economic improvements.

As a rule, the market is the product of a long evolution. However, backward countries that intend to speed up the growth process and have a market founded on inadequate legal institutions can reform it in a relatively short time by profiting from the experiences of the now advanced countries.

A problem of this kind also appears, with peculiar characteristics, in the former socialist countries that have started a process of transition from centrally planned to market economies. Up to now it does not seem that their strategy has been wise. Certainly it has not been wise in the case of the countries of the Former Soviet Union (FSU), that implanted a centrally planned system much sooner than the other countries of the Soviet Bloc and had much more rudimentary market institutions than, for example, the countries of Eastern Europe, that became socialist much later and as a consequence of foreign military occupation.

Agricultural development

For all underdeveloped countries, but particularly for those where poverty is increasing, the priority is for measures necessary to promote *agricultural development*.

In discussing the causes of the prosperity of the American colonies, Adam Smith, as we saw in chapter 1, emphasized the fact that in those colonies, not fettered by remnants of feudal institutions, land was plentiful and free: 'the cost of a piece of land consists almost exclusively in the operations necessary for making it suitable for cultivation'. Then, paraphrasing the title of Arthur Lewis' famous 1954 article, for countries of this type it is possible to envisage a process of 'Economic development with unlimited supply of land'. In fact, in several underdeveloped countries land, in comparison with population, is unlimited nor are there, properly speaking, any feudal fetters left. It is true that in Africa and in Asia certain colonial powers introduced private property of land in their own interest (estates or plantations); but it is also true that this often refers only to limited areas, especially near the coast. Even now the rule is the availability of free land, although often, owing to the necessity of organizing simple systems of irrigation, making pieces of land suitable for cultivation can be very costly and requires an intervention by the state or by local communities. In any case, in countries where the supply of land is 'unlimited', the expansion of cultivation often proceeds irrationally from the social point of view (often, deforestation is the result) and in several countries agricultural output increases more slowly than population (see chapter 6, p. 125). The reason is that the availability of land is only one of the conditions necessary for the growth of production. Another very important condition – strictly speaking, a prior condition – is to establish a tolerable degree of *security* in the countryside, so that those who intend to organize productive units can have a reasonable probability of enjoying the fruits of their investment (this need was also acutely felt in England at the beginning of modern times). A third condition is the degree of *education* of the people and a certain knowledge of simple techniques of agriculture.

There is a fourth condition emphasized by Smith, concerning the legal framework. Since private property of land in certain underdeveloped countries is the exception, not the rule, the question arises whether it is convenient to introduce it as the rule, on the assumption that the property of land is an essential condition of agricultural development. In fact, it is not true that private property of land is a 'natural' state of affairs. In certain stages of the social evolution, and even now in large parts of the underdeveloped world, the rule is some type of communal property, the village being the nucleus. In Europe, in feudal times, all lands belonged to the king or to aristocratic landlords, but there were important areas for the common use of peasants – the so-called 'commons' (see chapter 2, p. 39). More recently, in Russia and China before their revolutions and in several underdeveloped countries, especially in Africa, a sort of communal property is widespread where an authority representing the families forming a village regulates the users' rights. In Mozambique, for instance, such an arrangement is still now widespread (and the conviction that this was the correct way of conducting agricultural activities so deeply penetrated the popular consciousness that peasants opposed the attempts of the socialist governments when, in the 1970s, they tried to organize rural cooperatives to become the owners of the land). At present, attempts are under way to introduce the individual property of land on a large scale. This seems to be an ill advised line of conduct: such an idea should be put aside, at least for the time being.

What is really important for agricultural development is not private property as such, but a reasonable certainty, for the cultivators, of enjoying in the course of time the fruits of the improvements that they introduce on the pieces of land on which they work. This can certainly be obtained when the cultivator is also the owner; but it can be obtained also in the case of long leases; and *long leases* can be granted either by private landowners, or by public or communal organizations. It seems that such a formula is now being studied in the countries of the FSU and that it has been successfully applied in contemporary China. It does not seem, however, that it has been considered in certain African countries. In order to promote agricultural development, it is probably advisable to adopt the formula of long leases granted to cultivators by the communal authority, endowed with the capacity of providing technical assistance, including simple means of production. (This formula is a special case of the third type of agrarian reform which I will discuss below.)

Recognizing that agriculture can be conducted either for family consumption or for the market, long leases should be construed differently in the two situations, and the differences should be relevant when technical assistance for the production and the commercialization of products is included in the programmes. Since the communal authority in charge of long leases is not interested in making profits, in a preliminary period each lease could be free; but in order to cover expenses, in the course of time a charge should be imposed. It is important to insert the reorganized communal authorities into the tradition of already-existing authorities, that have always administered the rights of users and changes of holders, owing to death, emigration and changes of activity.

There are other distinctions to be made, such as between the formal and informal sector in rural and in urban areas. As I have already noted, a shift of firms from the informal to the formal sector is favourable to the growth process. In under-developed countries, the policy of long leases granted by communal authorities can help such a shift, which requires the gradual enlargement of the land register for rural as well as for urban areas.

These observations apply to several important countries, particularly in Africa. In other countries, especially in Latin America, the problem of accelerating agricultural development is still important, but their traditions are more similar to those of Western countries. In these countries it is advisable to think about *agrarian reforms.*

There are at least three types of agrarian reforms:

- The first belongs to the *traditional type*, of which the core is represented by the redistribution of land, especially large estates, with secondary attention to collateral measures, such as a supply of water to the peasants, technical assistance, certain means of production and credit on easy conditions.
- The second type is a reform in which the importance of the collateral measures just mentioned is not inferior to the *redistribution of land.*
- The third type, which I will call the Smithian type, is the reform of *agrarian contracts* in the direction recommended by Smith – that is, that the fruits of the improvements introduced by the cultivator, who is not necessarily the owner, be reaped wholly or almost

wholly by him alone (Smith, 1961 [1776], book III, ch. II). This result can be obtained, first of all, by long leases, but also by introducing appropriate rules. This type of reform has the advantage of producing results very similar to those which can be obtained through the other two types of reforms, but meeting with much less serious political resistance than an expropriation is likely to provoke. This type of reform has been silently introduced in several countries, among them Italy, with favourable results – aided, we must add, by the general development of the economy, which promoted emigration from the countryside to the towns, a rising trend of agricultural wages and a falling trend in agricultural rents. The idea is to introduce such a reform not piecemeal, but on the basis of systematic programme.

The promotion of small firms in rural areas and in industrial districts

In the new stage of modern capitalism the relative weight of employment in small firms in total employment has increased in all advanced countries since, in these new conditions, small size is no longer a reason for inferiority and in certain activities can even represent an advantage. I have already pointed out that such a change is favourable to the underdeveloped countries, whose market, owing to low *per capita* income, is necessarily limited and, therefore, not favourable to large firms, whose size is caused by economies of scale.

Small firms can occur either in industrial districts, on the periphery of towns, or scattered in rural areas. Giorgio Fuà (who has studied this question in depth, not only theoretically, but through fieldwork in a region of Central Italy; Fuà, 1988), points out that not only in the past, but even in our own time in certain Italian regions, especially in the Centre and in the North East, the process of industrialization for a

series of reasons, started in rural areas. In fact, small industrial firms were created by farmers who, thanks to the development of communications and by exploiting existing
infrastructures 'inherited from history' were able to begin the
new activities without incurring great expense and sold their
goods not only in local markets but increasingly in distant
markets and abroad. Often the new firms were created by
younger members of the families who, owing to technical
progress in agriculture, were no longer necessary for the cultivation. Yet, the older members continued to work in agriculture, thus providing subsistence for the whole family. If
the family had a tradition of craft specialization of one type
or another, as is common in the regions of Central Italy, and
if its members had a non-negligible degree of education, then
the favourable conditions were present to start an industrial
activity, modest at first, but capable of developing in the
course of time. The cost of production was low since the producers' cost of living was low, owing to advantages concerning lodging and foodstuff, two of the main items of such cost.
In the course of time, however, the older members of the families retired, so that one of the advantages (foodstuff) disappeared. This, together with the gradual growth of family
firms, might induce people to move towards the periphery of
towns, where they could take advantages of a number of services. This implies an expansion of industrial areas near
towns, that might develop into true industrial districts (see
Becattini, 1998, ch. III, sec. 4).

The agglomeration of firms in industrial districts gives rise
to a variety of external economies, among which is the ease
with which firms can find the intermediate goods and services
necessary for their production and the rapid diffusion of information concerning markets and new simple technologies.

The previous observations arise out of the experience of
Central Italian regions. In underdeveloped countries the
government, in order to promote the creation of small industrial firms in rural areas and in industrial districts, has to

reduce bureaucratic regulations to a minimum, to build up or strengthen specific infrastructures and to organize a system of education and of formation to favour the diffusion of innovations, also through cooperation with the universities; such innovations can well be very modest from the technological standpoint, but are very important in a process of growth. In underdeveloped countries, an important role can be played by centres for the formation of technicians and experts, such as those mentioned in chapter 9 (see p. 179). Districts should be founded on three bases: specific infrastructures, formation of workers and diffusion of innovations, with only one office for all bureaucratic functions.

In developed countries, too, small firms can have various advantages. In the case of small firms in rural areas, as we have seen, these advantages refer first of all to lodging and foodstuff. More generally, small firms get advantages in terms of labour costs, since their dependent workers very seldom strike to compel their masters to pay higher wages; the master himself is, after all, a worker similar to them, with the function of a leader (in such circumstances, the Marxian class struggle is not relevant); wages rise when productivity increases and when the leader finds it necessary not to lose his workers, who might be tempted to leave his firm if they could obtain higher incomes elsewhere, perhaps giving rise to new firms.

If we consider the advantages of small firms and of the self-employed, the different behaviour of employment of dependent and of independent workers in certain industries appears unsurprising (see chapter 5, p. 103): employment has declined in the former subsector, mainly owing to the competition of underdeveloped countries, where wages are a fraction of those of developed countries, whereas it has increased in the subsector of independent workers.

Especially after the Second World War several underdeveloped countries adopted a policy of industrialization, not so much by promoting industrial districts, but more often by promoting the creation of large private and public firms. To this end the governments of those countries have introduced tariff protection and subsidies of various kinds. Such a policy was motivated by several reasons, two in particular. First, the growth of manufacturing industry is often associated with a sustained process of growth – probably in the minds of political leaders there was a '*post hoc ergo propter hoc*' type of reasoning. Second, development of industry, particularly of heavy industry, was considered to be fundamental, not only for economic growth but also for the production of modern weapons – i.e. for military reasons. The prestige of the government had also to be considered, a prestige connected with the reasons just mentioned.

The economic reasons put forward in favour of a policy of industrialization supported by the state, mainly through tariff protection, have been severely criticized by several economists, beginning with Quesnay and Smith. In practice, since the Second World War the political leaders of certain countries (South Korea, Taiwan and Singapore) have followed Quesnay's and Smith's recommendations; others, such as the countries of the Indian subcontinent, have preferred instead Colbertian policies (Eltis, 1988), caused also, after the Second World War, by the influence of the Soviet Union that carried out from the beginning a policy of forced development of heavy industry, initially to create the basis for the production of modern armaments.

Closely related to the problem of tariff protection of investment goods, we find the question of the ratio between wages and the prices of machinery. Protection brings about an increase of the denominator and therefore a decrease in this ratio. As we have seen (chapter 3, p. 68), this blunts an important impulse behind the increase of productivity. Moreover, it is likely that a developing country will not have well equipped research laboratories comparable to those of advanced countries. This means that the protected production of machinery prevents the use of more efficient machinery imported from advanced countries. All this implies a serious brake on the process of growth.

There is a second negative consequence of the high prices of investment goods caused by tariff protection: the investment/income ratio, taken as an approximate index of the saving ratio, becomes misleading, since to some extent the numerator (investment) is artificially swollen by the prices of investment goods inflated by tariff protection. Thus, a policy tending to push up the propensity to save is partly frustrated, since a share of saving is wasted (Sylos Labini, 1990).

Environmental problems arising from poverty, and those arising from opulence

Most people believe that the environmental problems of the world arise principally from the advanced countries, whereas the responsibility of underdeveloped countries is deemed to be marginal. This is not really so. It is true that the environmental problems depending on gas emissions, especially carbon dioxide, can be attributed mainly to industrial countries – cars, residential and industrial heating, energy-intensive industrial sectors, thermoelectric power generation and so on. But the same problems are increasingly present in developing countries and in the formerly centrally planned ones, with the additional problem that as a rule these countries cannot afford the more expensive 'clean' technologies which are increasingly being used in advanced countries, where environmental regulations are ever-more severe.

Particular environmental problems arising from underdeveloped countries are caused by deforestation and desertification, phenomena no less disastrous than gas emissions. As we have seen, deforestation depends on two main causes – poverty and unbridled speculation carried out by unscrupulous businessmen, whom we could almost label criminals.

Normally businessmen, both in advanced and in underdeveloped countries, pollute the air and poison ground or underground water if this swells their profits. But other businessmen can make profits by producing anti-pollution appliances. Some new technologies tend to aggravate pollution; but the appliances intended to reduce pollution are also the result of new technologies. We have to recognize that many of the problems originated by technical progress can be solved by technical progress itself: incentives, taxes and prohibitions from the state can help. Such measures can help even more if they are supplemented by interventions intended to stimulate dynamic competition among firms to reduce pollution at decreasing cost.

Until President Reagan, the United States was among the world leaders in anti-pollution measures. In the *Economic Report of the President* for 1982 (pp. 114–15), the first signed by Ronald Reagan, capital expenditures for pollution abatement were considered one of the possible causes, although a secondary one, of the productivity slowdown.

In any case, under Reagan the introduction of anti-pollution measures was reduced. It is true, however, that the Reagan as well as the Bush Administrations introduced 'tradable emission rights', which have had a remarkable success. This means that market forces can be channelled in the right direction by the state, which has the main responsibility in this area. Here the market mechanism works very badly: well devised regulations, many of them included in international agreements, are necessary, since the living conditions of the whole world are at stake.

For environmental problems, internal and international regulations are thus necessary, and can be usefully combined with devices imitating certain market mechanisms, such as tradable emission rights. This combination can be applied to all activities in which a free and unfettered market gives rise to negative results. Thus fiscal measures conditioning market mechanisms or rules similar to those followed in auction sales or competitive devices, based on objective standards, to be adopted in public structures – for instance, public hospitals – should be seriously considered.

To a large extent, we find energy at the heart of environmental problems, the driving force of modern economic development. A methodological criterion adopted by several economists and international institutions consists in estimating the *shadow costs* of traditional sources of energy, such as coal, oil and gas – including, besides market prices, the costs attributable to pollution and other environmental damage. These costs should be compared with those, actual and foreseeable, of alternative sources of energy, as they become available. Since the costs attributable to pollution are very uncertain, it is best to estimate conventionally the minimum indicative costs after consulting a variety of experts, and inquiries of this type are already under way (see the *World Development Report*, 1993, pp. 96–8). These shadow costs would represent standards of reference with which to gauge the expediency of producing or stimulating the use of new sources of energy, including, among the costs, investment in research. As for traditional sources, these shadow costs would also be useful to assess the expediency of introducing new taxes at national and international levels to put a brake on the use of polluting sources of energy and to stimulate the use of newer sources. A well devised taxation policy could accelerate the reduction, already under way, of energy intensity – i.e. of the energy/GNP ratio.

One remark on the productivity slowdown in the United States in the early 1980s; the 1993 *World Development Report* honestly admitted that only half of the slowdown could be explained statistically. In such conditions, even a limited weight assigned in the explanation to the expenditures for pollution abatement was out of place. Departing from mainstream economics and adopting a line recalled in chapter 3 (p. 69), I have shown that the productivity slowdown can be explained very satisfactorily without any recourse to expenditures for pollution abatement (Sylos Labini, 1990, pp. 211–12). This shows how unfortunate the practical consequences of bad theoretical analysis can be. It is to be hoped that, after a long intermission, the United States can resume leadership in world anti-pollution strategy.

For the future a nightmare is often evoked: if the underdeveloped countries entered into a sustained process of economic growth following a path similar to that of the now advanced countries – mass production of traditional cars, polluting factories and the rest – then a catastrophic outcome would be in sight for the whole of mankind. We hope that certain innovations – for instance, electric cars – can dispel that nightmare. Another very important contribution can be made by that type of industrialization that has asserted itself in certain parts of Europe, especially in Central Italy, led by industrial–rural districts and, on a much more extensive scale, in China. The relatively small units characterizing these districts can avoid large polluting factories, with advantages also for the workers, since in these units the terrible suffering connected with mass production and alienation can be largely avoided. Thus, it is important for everyone to promote the spread of this type of industrialization in underdeveloped countries.

9

The problem of corruption

The reform of public administration, corruption and the three types of districts

The reform of public administration appears to be the precondition of any reform. In the epoch of colonies, it was in the interest of the dominating power to organize a highly centralized administrative system more efficiently to control the colony, militarily and economically. With the decolonization process no important change has occurred in the organization of public administration, except that the white colonists have been substituted by natives. But the new bosses are no better than the previous ones; in a sense they are worse, since the abuse of the latter found limits in the colonial offices of their mother country. True, the abuses committed by the central governments of the colonial countries were very serious and corruption was widespread. But the hope was that, with independence and self-government, the cases of corruption would diminish. This has not been so.

Before discussing the present-day situation, it is fitting to recall that in India corruption assumed appalling dimensions during the eighteenth century, owing also to the disastrous influence of the East India Company, which was closely connected with the British political authority, a corruption that was infecting the mother country as well. But towards the end of that century there occurred a reaction, led by Edmund Burke, which quickly reversed the trend, both in India and in

Great Britain and from this point of view the situation improved in both countries, especially in Great Britain (Adonis, 1997).

In our own time, we are justified on the whole in thinking that, with decolonization, corruption did not diminish but, on the contrary, probably increased, since the natives who entered into public administration had a quasi-monopoly of education. And in a society of illiterates, people who enjoy a quasi-monopoly of education tend to exploit it. Corruption can have paralysing effects on the very start of the process of economic growth. Indeed, corruption in the public administration of many underdeveloped countries is very serious. In keeping with the historical interpretation of the great differences among populations, this fact can in no way be explained in racial terms. Yet, those who recognize that this is the situation can be gripped by a sense of deep frustration and even of despair, since a corrupt public administration is not capable of introducing, not to mention administering, the necessary reforms.

As an antidote to despair, we have to study a strategy aimed at reducing to a minimum the central public administration, reducing it to a nucleus devoted only to public order and justice, attributing the task of fulfilling most of the communal services to the districts of the three types mentioned in chapter 8, formed around villages. The idea is to dismantle as soon as possible the majority of central bureaux and their local branches, often an inheritance of the old colonial times or of more recent statist experiments – in certain cases of a Marxist brand. To decentralize the management of the communal services on the basis of very simple rules means to bring the control of common interests within the reach of poor and largely illiterate people; this is easy, since in each village people know each other and therefore misbehaviour and abuse is much reduced or even rendered impossible. This highlights the vital importance of action against mass illiteracy for starting a strategy of reforms based on simple democratic foundations and on self-government; this can give rise to vigorous economic growth with a view, in the long run, to a sustained process of civic development.

In each district an office seems to be necessary for supplying technical advice, formed by very few people elected in each community – these people should be trained in centres organized in the capital of the country or in the advanced countries, with the proviso that officials themselves will go and visit peasants, artisans and small industrialists rather than vice versa.

The use of the surplus: self-financing, credit, taxes and price control in underdeveloped countries

The preliminary conditions for a process of growth are (a) the existence of a surplus over the production of the means of subsistence for producers and the reconstitution of the means of production and (b) the productive use of at least a part of that surplus. The productive use of the surplus can be carried out fundamentally in four ways: (1) from a decision of the producer himself – what in a modern firm is defined as 'self-financing', (2) through a transfer via credit, (3) via taxes and (4) via price controls. It is well to remember that in all cases an intention is one thing, results another. However, especially in the case of credit for consumption or fiscal transfers, an unproductive use can already be found in the intention – loans can be granted to consumers and fiscal revenue can be used for military purposes or for social transfers: the latter can be productive in a broad, not in a narrow sense.

The second channel – that is, credit – deserves special attention. In each district, a credit institution should be promoted, for facilitating loans to independent workers and to microfirms. It is well to reflect on the experience of the Grameen Bank, created by a Bangladesh economist, Muhammad Yunus, who had been a pupil of Nicholas

Georgescu Roegen in the United States (Yunus, 1997). The bank was organized in the form of a cooperative and spread in many countries, mainly underdeveloped ones, but also in the poor sections of advanced countries. At present the Grameen Bank has many millions of associates and can boast that the rate of repayment of loans is far higher than that of ordinary banks – 98 per cent or more. The principles governing the Bank are very simple: the amount of each loan is, as a rule, very modest; loans are granted, individually, to groups of five persons, preferably women, who are jointly responsible for the repayment of their debts; real guarantees, documents and bureaucratic paperwork are not requested – and we all know that these are the three great obstacles that make the access to credit to independent workers and small firms so difficult; finally, it is not the customers that have to go to the bank, but the bank employees who go to the customers. The Grameen Bank is an important innovation, that deserves a careful study. In my judgement, it is important not only from the purely economic standpoint but, by helping poor people to start small initiatives that can subsequently grow, promotes self-reliance and dignity. Moreover, by preferring women to men, considered more reliable as debtors because they often also have small children to raise, this experience can make a relevant contribution towards eroding the state of inferiority of women that is often found in underdeveloped countries. Even in advanced countries, a bank of this kind can be used to combat usury.

Each of the loans granted by a bank of the Grameen type is very small. For loans of a larger amount we should consider unions of banks and of firms, since such unions can reduce the risk on both sides and therefore can permit a reduction in the rate of interest as well as giving guarantees and carrying out bureaucratic functions.

The fiscal problem is very important, too, first of all in the promotion of a process of growth, through facilitating infrastructure building; secondly, fiscal revenue can be used for social purposes, mainly education and health; finally, a reduction in the use of that revenue for military purposes – in Third World countries, military expenses are often much larger than welfare expenses: it seems that to kill is more important than to live.

In Third World countries, especially in the low-income category, fiscal reform is very necessary. Here more than in other cases, however, we have to try and abandon the biases implicit in our Western mentality. If invited to present their recommendations, Western economists should recommend, first of all, a careful study of the economic and social situation of the country concerned, with the idea of exploiting local traditions as much as possible, especially if they are old and therefore deeply rooted.

Second, Adam Smith's four maxims (see the introduction, p. 4) have to be considered; the problem that deserves special attention is the one referred to in the fourth maxim – i.e. the most convenient way to collect taxes. Often, in those countries, export duties have a significant weight; this appears irrational, since exports are to be encouraged, not hindered. Yet, the rationale of those duties is that it is relatively easy to collect them; it is certainly advisable to substitute them, but only after devising workable alternatives. (Among these, we find indirect taxes; yet, we should not forget that an increase of such taxes tends to be inflationary.)

Third, when tax revenue can be directly connected with particular services, such as certain educational and health services, an effort should be made to specify that connection to all interested people.

The fact that a good proportion of fiscal receipts depends on exports, and particularly on exports of certain raw materials, renders those receipts vulnerable to variations in the terms of trade, which often move against producers. This gives rise to a dangerous linkage between fiscal receipts, the capacity of importing foreign goods and the ability of servicing foreign debt.

The variations in fiscal receipts tend also to affect welfare expenses. The role of such expenses in the process of growth should never be underrated: these expenses are not a luxury and saving on them, by a programme of cutting the public deficit, can prove to be a very serious mistake. Thus, in Tanzania financial cutbacks were introduced during the 1980s in several social services such as education and health; in a very short time a deterioration had taken place in education as well as in infant mortality, in the death rate and in life expectancy at birth (Basu and Morrissey, 1997, pp. 173–6). In view of this, it is advisable to make a great effort to decentralize the organization and financing of health services. When I visited Sri Lanka, it seemed to me that such a decentralization had been to some extent carried out: I noticed simple infirmaries even in small villages.

In any case, the lesson that we can draw from the Tanzanian experience is that cutbacks in the expenses of education and health, even in the short run, can be harmful for welfare and, in the long run, harmful for the growth process itself. The IMF and the World Bank should be very careful in imposing heavy conditions for a rapid reduction of public deficit; such a reduction should be gradual and should not hurt welfare expenses.

A fiscal reform suitable for several African countries is by necessity very different from the reforms suitable for middle-income countries. Thus, in Latin American countries a fiscal reform is certainly needed to accelerate the growth process and to make it more secure, but in these countries such a reform should centre on direct taxation since, as already hinted, an increase in indirect taxes and tariffs, when they apply to large masses of consumers, is inflationary. Naturally, direct taxes are to be differentiated in favour of firms' investment. In these countries a strategy for accelerating growth should include, besides a reform of taxation, a reform of agrarian contracts and a package of investment in specific infrastructures to create or strengthen the industrial districts.

A government can extract a part of the surplus not only via taxes but also via price control. This has been tried by compelling peasants to deliver their products to a public pool at low prices and then selling them at higher prices and channelling the surplus extracted to finance industrial growth. This was the policy adopted by the Soviet Government in the 1930s. Such a policy can have some success, but it is disastrous in the long run, not only because it blocks the growth of agriculture which in underdeveloped countries should have first priority, but also because that strategy is bound to be largely frustrated, since peasants will try by all means not to deliver their products to the state and will increase their self-consumption and barter with the products of other peasants and of persons outside agriculture.

National and local public works

I insisted earlier on the necessity for low-income countries that intend to initiate or to accelerate a growth process to rely on local communities and to reduce to a minimum the tasks attributed to the central government, not for the sake of a doctrinaire *laissez-faire* philosophy, but because public administrations in former colonies as a rule present an unhappy mixture of inefficiency and corruption. This guideline runs counter to the traditional line, according to which public works of national significance are as a rule decided by national governments on the basis of agreements between the government of the underdeveloped country and that of the advanced country which finances a given public work, and indicates which firms will carry it out. Every underdeveloped country needs certain fundamental public works of national importance, first of all in the field of transport such as highways, railways, airports, harbours and telecommunications, but also in the field of power facilities and water supply. Considering that, under these circumstances, corruption can be actually enhanced, even among political and economic circles in advanced countries, and since public works of national importance cannot be entrusted to local communities, we have to look for another solution. Probably the best way is to entrust the realization of public works of this type to an international agency financed by advanced countries, entering into agreements with the governments of underdeveloped countries and establishing regulations capable of enhancing the efficiency and the rapidity of the process. The international agency could be promoted either by the United Nations or, in the case of Africa, by the European Union. The situation is different in the case of public works of local importance. Here, the guidelines mentioned above can be adopted, with the necessary adaptations.

Two centres for the formation of experts for underdeveloped countries and a centre for medical services

Nowadays the conviction is widespread that the assistance that advanced countries can extend to underdeveloped countries for promoting their economic growth should not be mainly financial, as it has been until recently; such assistance should consist essentially in *real services*. Thus, if we refer to poor African countries, one of the first problems is to supply organizational assistance for developing the three districts – rural, industrial and mixed – on the basis of traditional local communities; the experts could be found in those European areas where such districts have already prospered for a long time. Since that in these districts credit and tax institutions of a simple type are necessary, experts in these fields can play an important role. As for credit, experts can be found, I think, by resorting to the headquarters of the Grameen Bank and of the World Bank. In the case of taxes, the experts are preferably to be found among administrators of local authorities of the advanced countries.

The reduction of foreign debts that the creditor countries

decide on from time to time is, no doubt, a relief, but little more than that. The advanced countries should accompany such reduction with positive actions, mainly in term of real services. Advanced countries and international organizations can play a very important role in four vital areas: medical services, education, rural technologies and, more generally, new technologies suited to developing countries.

We should emphasize two recommendations here. First, we must study the previous evolution and the present conditions of each country, to understand its traditions: reforms and changes must be compatible with them. Second, if it is true that not all that the Europeans did in the past was misguided, then we must study the past experiences of cooperation, public and private, lay and religious (the missions), to try to recover and develop what was positive and vital in those experiences – it is in fact by no means negligible.

All economists agree that to raise the level of education is essential for promoting growth in underdeveloped countries. Demographers emphasize the importance of reducing the illiteracy of women which, as we have seen, is one of the main factors governing the birth rate: the lower the degree of women's illiteracy, the lower the birth rate. After more than a century of hot discussion, in which we have seen Marxists allied to intellectuals belonging to different religions arguing in favour of unfettered demographic growth, almost all scholars at present recognize that a high demographic pressure tends to work against the improvement in living standards. It is, therefore, fundamental to try all means to accelerate the decline in the birth rate.

A great experiment could be tried if the European countries agreed to launch an organic programme for eradicating illiteracy in Africa, giving first priority to women's illiteracy in the African countries, since many of these countries present the most serious instances of poverty. The World Bank has already made important interventions in this field; the experience thus accumulated should be exploited to the maximum. A European centre for supervising the realization of this programme of education is strongly recommended.

As for the organization of rural and industrial districts in Africa, another centre should be created in Europe for the formation of experts. A third centre should concern the coordination of medical services.

The three centres should include very few people: their task would be only that of coordinating and advising the units in Africa organized in the three main European languages in common use – French, English and Portuguese (this is the suggestion of Massimo Cresta). Clearly, the creation of the three centres and of the local units for education and the formation of panels of rural and industrial experts would imply a great financial and organizational effort. But this seems to be the only alternative to purely financial aid, which has been both costly and disastrous and a source of corruption for both the donor and the receiving countries.

Economists have pointed out that scientific and technical progress gives rise to technologies that as a rule have economic and social justifications for the advanced countries, where most of the laboratories are located. It is important to stimulate the development of technologies compatible with the traditions and suited to the particular needs of underdeveloped economies. By exploiting the modern electronic technologies, however, and with the cooperation of universities and academies in advanced countries as well as the great international institutions, it should be possible to organize a network for a world research programme, which would give due importance to the economic, demographic and medical problems of underdeveloped countries, the problem of migration and of the environment that concern all the countries of the world. There are already interesting ties among academies, universities and international institutions working in these fields; what is needed, however, is a unified organization (Sylos Labini, 1992b). Modern communication systems make all this much easier than in the past.

It is certainly important to promote the production of new technologies relevant for underdeveloped countries through the cooperation of advanced countries and their diffusion through an international network. But it is even more important to multiply, on a systematic basis, the research institutions and the centres for the formation of research workers within the underdeveloped countries themselves, beginning with the poorest.

If it is true that the great challenge of the twenty-first century is the development of the Third World, then an increasing number of scholars, scientists and political leaders must concentrate their efforts in this direction. To promote the three centres, even if restricted to Africa, and a network for a world research programme, the United Nations and the European Union should probably organize an international conference and create a sort of permanent committee to prepare and advise on the main lines of a strategy of reforms by utilizing the research work carried out by international institutions, universities and research facilities: the patrimony of accumulated knowledge is very large indeed. But it needs coordination to make further developments both more efficient and more rapid.

Conclusion: a strategy for reform

Revolution and reform

'The sleep of the reason breeds monsters.' But the trouble is
not with sleeping reason, but with ends – the ends chosen by
intellectuals and political leaders, who in certain countries
were able to seize power after convincing a good number of
their people that those ends were worth pursuing at all costs;
as a rule, the means adopted were fully rational. In fact, the
systems of ideas – the ideologies – of those intellectuals and
of those leaders had some of the characteristics of a religious
faith. This is true in the case of Karl Marx, who preached the
necessity of a proletarian revolution by arguing – and this is
one of his great responsibilities – that the civilized way of
reform to solve social problems, even the most difficult ones,
was largely impracticable. His other great responsibility was
his formula 'the dictatorship of the proletariat', which was
based on an imperfect analysis and was used to make the
most ruthless dictatorships intellectually respectable. The
right-wing Nazi ideology, too, was a kind of faith, even if
Adolf Hitler's cultural level was significantly more modest
than that of Karl Marx (*Mein Kampf* is in no way comparable
with *Das Kapital*). Hitler preached that the historical task of
the Germans, as members of a superior race, was to dominate
the world, eliminating the inferior races – in a mass ethnic
cleansing – or transforming them into slaves.

Communism and Nazism cannot be put on the same plane,

however. Communism goes back to one of the noblest aspirations of man, Nazism and its ideological core, racism, embodies one of the most barbarous passions, the love of man to oppress or to kill his fellow man in the name of a supposed racial superiority. Yet, 'the way to Hell is paved with good intentions' and the Communist dictatorship was no better than the Nazi dictatorship, concentration camps included.

Marx's doctrine was addressed to countries that could be classified as 'advanced' even in his time. Elsewhere (Sylos Labini, 1974) I have tried to show how Marx, contradicting the logic of his own analysis, eventually convinced himself that his doctrine could be applied to a backward country such as Russia, where he found very capable followers among intellectuals, who thought that by building on the traditions of village communities in which land was held in common, 'society can skip a stage of history – the destructive, individualizing, capitalist stage' (Berg, 1964, p. 551). A similar thought occurred to several intellectuals and political leaders in Africa and Asia.

Here it is fitting to point out that in Russia revolution originated from a military defeat, not from social conflict. In the conditions of 1917 the abolition of the private property of the means of production did not represent the traumatic deed that it would have been in an advanced country: principally, it meant the abolition of the private property of the estates of the landed aristocracy. Small owners were limited in number; they were the heirs of the serfs, formally abolished shortly before the Bolshevik revolution. Moreover, they had obtained rights of possession of pieces of land previously held by village communities. At the beginning of the revolution, 'rich peasants' – the kulaks – were tolerated then, after 1929, persecuted and exterminated. Village communities were forcibly transformed into state farms or, more often, into cooperatives, although tiny pieces of land were left to a number of peasants. Even today property rights of land and of other means of production are considered with a sort of moral disapproval or at least with suspicion by the populations of the countries of the former Soviet Bloc, which is one of the important reasons for the difficulties that the expansion of the market economy is meeting in those countries.

Through Russia, Marxism gave rise to the great illusion in many backward countries that it was possible to find a short-cut from backwardness to a modern society. Thus Marxism became the doctrine of the hope for many of the poorest countries. Until recently, the high price paid by Russia was only partially known; most people were vaguely aware that it was high, but the idea prevailed among the Communists and the pro-Communists outside Russia that the price was worth paying in order to arrive in a relatively short time at a situation of wealth, power and equality.

That was an illusion, as nowadays is only too evident. And 'the damned of the Earth' after the experiment found themselves even more damned than before. Those people lived mostly in African and Asian countries. In such countries, central planning was not even tried or was tried by creating a bureaucratic organization that influenced only the limited sector of the economy controlled by the state. Instead, a policy of price controls was enforced, based on the idea of extracting a surplus from the agricultural sector to finance industrial development, with disastrous results.

Cuba and China are very special cases. Before Fidel Castro, Cuba was very backward and was brutally exploited in various ways by the United States, supporting a corrupt dictatorship led by Batista. The Cuban revolt was understandable and the first steps of the Castro dictatorship can be judged positively: illiteracy was drastically reduced and significant measures in favour of health in all strata of society introduced. But this should not blind us to the fact that Castro's regime was and still is a dictatorship. There are still political prisoners and, after the largely successful struggle against illiteracy, the educational system and cultural evolution did not make much progress. After a relatively short period economic development practically came to a standstill and the Cuban economy became heavily dependent on Soviet aid. Very soon the dictatorship became a barrier towards the progress of civilization; with the lack of freedom research activities suffered severely.

Similar remarks apply to China which, for the time being, is growing rapidly. At present China is certainly a dictatorship, but its social system cannot be defined as 'Communist' in any meaningful sense of the word. Moreover, as I observed in the Introduction (pp. 9–10), the growth process will meet with increasing difficulties if China is not able to introduce political freedom.

It has been said that in the historical challenge between Communism and Capitalism, the former failed and the latter won. To make this statement correct, it has to be amended and qualified in important ways. There are two main amendments. First, in advanced countries Communism has not even been tried – apart from the short-lived attempt made by Béla Kun in Hungary after the First World War; it has been carried out in underdeveloped countries, beginning with Russia, and in those relatively developed countries of Eastern Europe that were unfortunate enough to become, for military reasons, satellites of the Soviet Union. In fact, the Communism that has failed is the one that was carried out in the Soviet Union. On the other side – and this is the second amendment – the Capitalism that has won is primarily that of the United States where, as I have emphasized more than once in this book, a great importance was attributed since the beginning of its history to both economic and cultural development. This tradition has been reinforced in recent times – before, during and after the Second World War – thanks to the scientists who escaped from the two catastrophic myths of Nazism and Communism. Their emigration to the United

States meant that gifts of extraordinary importance were offered the two dictatorships; without such gifts it is doubtful whether the Allied Powers could have won the Second World War and, subsequently, the Cold War. Even now the strength of the United States comes not so much from their material resources as from their cultural wealth.

The Puritan tradition has also helped – there are several indications that corruption is much less widespread in the United States, at least at the level of central administration, than in many other civilized countries. And corruption is by no means a merely moral affair: if in backward countries it can have paralysing consequences on growth, in advanced countries it pollutes relations among individuals, who gradually lose their sense of dignity, and it tends to seriously damage the international image of the country concerned and in the long run, these 'intangibles' are much more important than 'tangibles'. In the long run, corruption can have paralysing effects in advanced countries, too, if it reaches universities and scientific organizations, as occurred in England in the eighteenth century – Adam Smith denounced the 'corruption' in some English universities (see Smith, 1961 [1776], book V, ch. I, part III, art. II). After a long and complex evolution, the trend in both political and academic life changed radically.

Institutional reform to create a growth-oriented market

The capitalist system, centred on the market in its various configurations, has undoubtedly proved to be a formidable engine of growth, provided it is coupled with political freedom and scientific research. Among the institutions constituting the capitalist system, we find private property of the means of production; the freedom to launch new enterprises; a great variety of organizational setups for economic activities – from the self-employed to large corporations; a growth-oriented system of contracts and of companies and a bankruptcy law. Among the institutions not properly 'capitalistic' but vitally conditioning its functioning, we find the school system, including universities and research organizations, and various types of non-profit institutions.

Little attention has been paid to the role, in the process of capitalist growth, of a well founded bankruptcy law. This law and several norms included in the system of contracts and of companies provides a safety net for entrepreneurs who launch new enterprises and carry out innovations by limiting the losses that could be incurred if such initiatives were not successful. Thus, the bankruptcy law and those norms that encourage risk-taking become essential. Socialist firms in a centrally planned economy were not allowed to fail – to go bankrupt – with the consequence that innovation was made very difficult, if not impossible. Therefore, it is not a paradox to say that 'capitalism' has 'won' first of all because its productive units could fail, whereas 'socialism' has lost because its productive units could not fail.

At present, the formerly socialist countries are in the process of transition from 'socialism' towards 'capitalism'. As I have already hinted, the preliminary reform is the creation of a growth-oriented market. To this end, advice given by economists alone can be simply disastrous, since most economists today know nothing, or almost nothing, of what, for the sake of brevity, I have called the 'Smithian approach', which gives owing weight to the institutional changes that cannot be seen as separate from the economic changes in the growth process.

After the abandonment of central planning in the former socialist countries, various Western economists gave the Russian government – let us take Russia as the reference country – several types of advice: to restore the market by abolishing all sorts of regulations, beginning with those concerning prices (as if, to restore the market, abolition of regulations was all that was needed); to reduce the public deficit by limiting expenses and raising taxes; to improve the balance of payments by modifying foreign exchange rates. Some of these measures have been suggested, or imposed, as conditions for granting external loans.

Such measures, taken one by one and in a short-run perspective, are often reasonable. But if we neglect the needs of a *coherent strategy of change* – of reform – that in the former socialist countries is absolutely essential, new troubles are likely to appear. Briefly, the approach suggested by these economists and their lack of interest in institutional and structural problems is bound to have disastrous effects. In the formerly socialist countries we find only wreckage of the old institutional system, while the new system is still to be developed and in any case is not functioning, also as a result of the wrong start in the reforms. The result has been an appalling increase in both poverty and corruption. It is not financial aid that such countries need most, but good advice in the design and the implementation of structures that can support and stimulate economic activity.

The best advice that we can give to the countries belonging until recently to the Soviet Bloc is to promote a preliminary study on the economic and institutional situation; on the basis of such a study it is fitting to combine economic and legal experts to devise systems of laws and rules capable of giving substance to the reforms necessary to promote growth. As for the institutional framework, considering the lack of orderly traditions in those countries, it is convenient to recommend the enactment of commercial codes similar to those that are in force in certain Latin countries. The imitation of such codes, with the necessary adaptations, can reduce to a minimum the time needed to carry out one of the most important institutional reforms.

It is fair to recognize that in the field of education the legacies of the former socialist countries in the transition seem to be positive. Yet, in the transition even in this field those countries are meeting with serious difficulties, probably owing to the insufficient flexibility of their educational systems and programmes. This problem, too, needs deep consideration.

The ideal of civic development

Having emphasized the importance of scientists escaping from Nazi, Fascist and Communist dictatorship going to the United States, a word needs to be said on Western scientists that, in the name of their Communist faith, emigrated to the Soviet Union, thus contributing to reduce the deep scientific gap between that country and Western countries, especially in the area of atomic energy development. Such scientists were much less numerous than those emigrating to the United States. Moreover – which is more important – the United States were (and are) enjoying an institutional and cultural milieu much more favourable to scientific development. In any case, the scientists emigrating to the Soviet Union showed that it is wrong to conceive of people as motivated only by selfishness and utilitarian interests. These scientists are an example of a passion that in many parts of the world induced a large number of persons to sacrifice their interests, and often even their life, for an ideal – better: for a faith. Eventually the Communist ideal failed tragically, but the human value of these people must be fully recognized.

All this is important for the strategy of reforms, since intellectual and political leaders must do their best to persuade the young that there are no shortcuts to the improvement of our common lot; particularly in their struggle with poverty, they must try to propose an ideal of civic development capable of exploiting those energies that were channelled in the wrong direction by the Communists. In this respect, the experience of Muhammad Yunus and of the Grameen Bank that he organized with a number of former left-wing extremists who became valid collaborators of his work (Yunus, 1997, ch. 18) is encouraging. The strategy of reforms is in any case not simply a technical affair: in under-developed countries it can succeed only if a sphere of the young feels deeply involved and identifies themselves with that strategy.

The appeal of the Communist faith and the moral poverty of Capitalism

Why, then, were so many people in so many countries attracted by the Communist ideal?

If we relate this question to large masses of people near subsistence level, the answer is easy: poverty is a very bad beast and for people to fight for Communism to overcome that poverty became a reason for living. At the same time, this battle was often for them a battle also for dignity and freedom, since the poor in one way or another are subordinated to rich or relatively rich people. The answer to that question is more difficult in the case of intellectuals, particularly if they are relatively rich: Intellectual pride? A guilty complex owing to their privileges – a sort of Croesus complex? Sympathy for their fellow human beings?

What is certain is that, if Capitalism is a formidable engine of growth, as a social system it is far from being ideal. It is true that free enterprise has stimulated initiative and self-reliance of individuals; but this applies mainly to small firms and to independent workers, it applies much less to those – both capitalists and workers – who operate within large firms. And the philosophy that 'money is what really matters' tends to prevail throughout society. Thus, richness in wealth is often accompanied by human and moral poverty, mainly transforming all values into market values. This, in the final analysis, is the reason of the appeal of the Communist faith and of other, transcendental, faiths opposed to Capitalism. However, it is fair to emphasize that the concentration of effort on money-hunting has made a decisive contribution to economic growth. And if it is true that

Capitalism is a formidable engine of growth then, in the long run, when growth and political action have given rise to a situation in which the needs of the whole society have been satisfied and poverty will be eradicated, an increasing number of people will be likely to abandon the now prevailing philosophy that makes money the most important aim of life; the economic problem has been solved and Capitalism, having fulfilled its historical task, will gradually fade away. In advanced countries the most serious non-economic problem is that wage earners are still subordinated, in one way or another, to the so-called 'capitalists', including top managers: whatever reduces this subordination implies a step forward in the direction of civic development. Firms require leadership, but this does not necessarily imply a sort of unacceptable microauthoritarianism: any measures are to be recommended that raise the position of wage earners – profit-sharing, participation in managerial decisions, including those concerning the organization and redistribution of labour made necessary by technical progress. After all, the relations between dependent workers and capitalists or managers are not the same all over the world: in the United States we find, on the one hand, excesses of individualism seldom accompanied by violence but, on the other, for historical reasons (see chapter 2, p. 37), we find relations much less authoritarian than in Europe, which contributes to explaining the scanty following of socialist movements in that country, if we except certain groups of European immigrants.

Capitalism as a system is compatible with both dictatorships and democratic regimes. Under certain cultural and ethnic conditions Capitalism has favoured the process of democratization which in our epoch tends to spread out all over the world amid all sorts of difficulties and tragedies. At present, however, economic growth and the creation of a robust democratic setup are still very serious problems for the majority of mankind.

In spite of its economic virtues, the capitalist system seems to have been incapable of eradicating poverty, even in the most advanced countries. However, it is high time that we admitted that Capitalism conditions, but does not cover, the whole society or the whole of society. A democratic regime leaves ample room, on the one hand, to independent intellectuals and, on the other, to non-profit activities and is composed of different parties that compete for votes and often, for this reason and to prevent social instability, exert much effort to combat poverty. The outcome can be – and in certain countries has been – positive, mainly owing to non-capitalist forces, i.e. forces outside the profit motive.

No doubt, people suffering in poverty see economic improvement as the most important of all aims. Yet, in interpreting the evolution of modern societies the so-called 'economic factor' has been grossly exaggerated, not only by Marx, but also by many other thinkers, both left- and right-wing.

Take, for instance, slavery, a phenomenon widespread for centuries all over the world, and even now far from having disappeared. After the discovery of the New World slavery underwent a new development, with the huge traffic of human beings from Africa towards Northern and Southern America, where in several regions colonizers organized capitalist systems embodying activities founded on slavery – another instance of the great variety of 'capitalisms'.

Smith emphasized that in modern times the economic advantages of slaves with respect to free labourers were less and less relevant, even in plantations, since slaves tended to exert the minimum effort and did not care to improve their abilities. Slavery survived longer than economic advantages could justify owing to the 'love to domineer' (Smith, 1961, [1776], book I, p. 412), which certainly does not enter into the area of economic motives properly understood. Today, there are new forms of slavery (Arlacchi, 1999), though in certain limited areas of Brazil slavery survives with features not very different from those of former times.

In general, ethnic and religious conflicts that are outside

the realm of economic motives appear to be far more important than economic conflicts. It is paradoxical that ethnic conflicts seem to be more frequent in the countries in which poverty is most serious and widespread. On the other hand, we notice ethnic conflicts also in advanced countries where the economic problem seems to be no longer the prime consideration. In fact, in advanced countries the problem of increasing *per capita* income is less and less important, whereas two problems have acquired increasing relevance: leisure and the quality of labour.

The solution to the economic problem

In the long run the increase in productivity, owing to innovations, translates itself to a large extent into a systematic increase in *per capita* income and partly into leisure, i.e. a reduction in working hours – very roughly: two-thirds and one-third, respectively, of the yearly rate of productivity increase. All indications are for a continuation of this trend, with the latter ratio gradually prevailing over the former, so that Keynes' prediction of a working week of 25 hours in a not too distant future (Keynes, 1970, [1930]) and subsequently even less is not so misleading. This applies to commodities, more and more being produced by automatic machines and robots, governed by intellectual workers: eventually manual workers will disappear and services will be the only production employing people.

With the increase of *per capita* income, employment as such has decreasing relevance, whereas the quality of labour and the satisfaction that can be obtained by the different kinds of jobs becomes more and more important. The *quality of labour*, which as a rule means the quality of life, depends first of all on scientific progress and on innovation, not merely because the number of scientists and research workers is growing, but principally because the new technologies and the new goods require an increasing number of technicians and highly skilled workers. The increase in the cultural level of workers allows an increasing participation in both the organization of their productive activities and the management of firms. The whole composition of the labour force is changing – I would say, improving – and the number of jobs capable of giving satisfaction to workers grows incessantly. At the same time, part-time employment should be vigorously encouraged, not only because such a policy can reduce unemployment but also because it favours the entry of women into the labour market, which contributes to their full emancipation.

The fact that for a few advanced countries the solution of the economic problem is in sight – if we except the shameful segments of poverty and non-negligible shares of youth unemployment – does not mean that such countries are entering into a state of bliss. Far from it: new problems are emerging, largely outside the economy, even more serious than the previous ones. The above picture applies to advanced, not to underdeveloped countries, in some of which the situation is not radically different from the one implicit in the Biblical prescription 'thou shalt earn thy bread with the sweat of thy brow'.

Overcoming underdevelopment: three European centres and the promotion of a world research programme

To help the underdeveloped countries, and especially the poorest of them, to enter into the spiral of economic and civic development is in the interest of all. However, the main effort needs to be exerted by advanced countries, even apart from the duty of human solidarity in their own interest, as at least two great problems – migration and environment – clearly show.

The large and increasing inflow of immigrants in the advanced countries will be the more advantageous for all countries the better is the health and cultural condition of the immigrants. On the other hand, the flow of immigrants needs to be managed in the interest of both the sending and the receiving countries, otherwise the algebraic sum of the advantages and the disadvantages is likely to be negative, at least for a time.

The problems caused by desertification and deforestation arise first of all in the countries of increasing poverty. What is at stake, however, is much more than this. With the progress of globalization the lot of mankind is becoming the same. And since revolutionary shortcuts have proved to be a tragic illusion, the only choice is a strategy of reform, bearing in mind that the development of underdeveloped countries should exploit their traditions, and its path cannot and should not be, as I have repeatedly emphasized, similar to that followed by the now advanced countries. True: such a strategy is a terribly complicated affair since the situations of the various underdeveloped countries are very differentiated and only a few general criteria can be singled out. True: in spite of their interest in the progress of underdeveloped countries, we cannot expect the major powers to support such a strategy out of sheer benevolence: a political or economic motive is necessary. Yet, we should realize that, if the decision centres of the major powers have often been led by people driven by the 'love to domineer', in other periods the leaders have been people who trusted their critical reason and thought in a long-run perspective. Sometimes such people succeed in gaining a significant cultural influence and a non-negligible decision-making power.

In any case, the task of adopting and carrying out a strategy of reform should be the concern of far-sighted intellectuals and political leaders in the countries concerned. In certain underdeveloped countries this is not a difficult problem; it is very difficult in several African countries. Intellectuals and leaders of that kind seems to be terribly few: besides Senghor of Senegal it is not easy to find others. Yet, the European

centres and, even more, the units that need to be organized
in several African regions for the creation of experts in education and technologies to be introduced in rural and industrial districts could in the long run aid the formation of
intellectuals of that type.

There are two conflicting views, widespread among even
cultivated people. According to the former, apart from a few
exceptions, a convergence is underway between the developed and underdeveloped countries. According to the latter
– apart, again, from a few exceptions – some countries are
becoming richer and richer and others are becoming poorer
and poorer. The analysis presented in this book shows that
both views are misleading: the picture is much more diverse
and complex.

For many underdeveloped countries the problem is that of
accelerating a development which is already underway, but
too slowly. Particular problems are represented by certain
underdeveloped countries, especially in Asia and in Central
America, where social and political conflicts have plagued
social and economic life for long periods. Other countries,
belonging to the former Soviet Bloc, are beset by the peculiar
problems of a long and difficult transition from a centrally
planned to a market economy. But the most serious, even dramatic, problems are those of Africa, especially Africa South
of the Sahara. Here, the main responsibility for supplying
support is that of the European countries, some of whom
were colonial powers in the continent.

In brief, efforts should be concentrated in five directions:

- First, to prepare a programme of basic infrastructures
  organized and financed, in agreement with the governments of underdeveloped countries, by the United
  Nations (or, in Africa, by the European Union).
- Second, a centre should be promoted for the coordination of medical services.
- Third, to launch a large programme of elementary

education, especially for women and, in Africa, under the supervision of a European centre.

- Fourth, to create another centre, again for Africa, for the formation of experts for the promotion of rural and industrial districts suited to the traditions of village communities but endowed with modern instruments and credit facilities; both centres should create locally operating units.

- Fifth, to promote higher education and research, particularly of research directed towards the specific problems of all underdeveloped countries, by exploiting all sorts of means, including modern electronic technologies. We have to reconsider the 1980 Brandt Report, now largely forgotten, by adopting the criterion of not stopping at financial allocations, but of transforming, whenever possible, financial assistance into organizational and real assistance.

All the developing countries represent a great challenge in the twenty-first century. But undoubtedly Africa is the top priority.

Bibliography

Adonis, A. (1997). 'Great Britain: The Civic Virtue on Trial', in D. Della Porta and Y. Mény (eds.), *Democracy and Corruption in Europe*, London: Pinter

Anghion, P. and Howitt, P. (1998). *Endogenous Growth Theory*, Cambridge, MA: MIT Press

Arcelli, M. (1962). *La funzione della produzione strumento per la programmazione*, Roma: ISCO

(1967). *Variazioni quantitative dei fattori e progresso tecnico*, Milan: Giuffrè

Arlacchi, P, (1999). *Schiavi – Il nuovo traffico di esseri umani*, Milan: Rizzoli

Associazione per lo sviluppo dell'industria nel Mezzogiorno (SVIMEZ) (1961). *Un secolo di statistiche italiane – Nord a Sud 1861–1961*, Roma: SVIMEZ

Baffigi, A., Pagnini, M. and Quintiliani, F. (1999). 'Industrial Districts: Do the Twins Ever Meet?', *Temi di discussione*, Servizio Studi, Banca d'Italia, Rome

Banca d'Italia (1998). *Relazione del Governatore*, Rome

Barro, R.J. and Sala-i-Martin, X. (1995). *Economic Growth*, New York: McGraw-Hill

Basu, P. and Morrissey, O. (1997). 'The Fiscal Impact of Adjustment in Tanzania in the 1980s', in C. Patel (ed.), *Fiscal Reforms in the Least Developed Countries*, Cheltenham: Edward Elgar

Baumol, W., Blackman, S.A. and Wolff, E.N. (1989). *Productivity and American Leadership: The Long View*, Cambridge MA.: MIT Press

Becattini, G. (1998). *Distretti industriali e made in Italy. Le basi socio-culturali del nostro sviluppo economico*, Turin: Borighieri-Bollati

Berg, E.J. (1964). 'Socialism in Tropical Africa', *Quarterly Journal of Economics'*, 77: 549–73

Brandt, W. (1980). *North–South: A Program for Survival*, New York: United Nations

Caffè, F. (1983). 'Un libro di Sylos Labini: c'è speranza per il Terzo mondo', *Rivista milanese di economia*, 6: 127–30

Caselli, G. (1994). 'Migrazioni internazionali', *Enciclopedia del Novecento*, XI, Rome: Istituto della Enciclopedia Italiano

Cattaneo, C. (1956). Del pensiero come principio d'economia pubblica', in A. Bertolino (ed.), *Scritti economici*, 3, Firenze: Le Monnier

Clark, C. (1940). *Conditions of Economic Growth*, London: Macmillan

De Long, J.B. and Summers, L.H. (1991). 'Equipment Investment and Economic Growth', *Quarterly Journal of Economics*, 106: 445–502

Domar, E.D. (1957). *Essays in the Theory of Economic Growth*, Oxford: Oxford University Press

Douglas, P. (1934). *The Theory of Wages*, New York: Macmillan
  (1967). 'Comments on the Cobb–Douglas Production Function', in M. Brown (ed.), *The Theory and Empirical Analysis of Production*, New York: National Bureau of Economic Research

Economic Report of the President (1982). Washington DC: Government Printing Office

Eltis, W. (1988). 'The Role of Industry in Economic Development: The Contrasting Theories of François Quesnay and Adam Smith', in K. Arrow (ed.), *The Balance between Industry and Agriculture in Economic Development*, 1, London: Macmillan for the International Economic Association: 175–97

Fortis, M. (1993). *Competizione tecnologica e sviluppo industriale. Fasi dell'economia mondiale dal 1850 al 1992*, Bologna: Il Mulino

Friedman, M. (1957). *A Theory of the Consumption Function*, Princeton: Princeton University Press

Frisch, R. (1965). *The Theory of Production*, Dordrecht: Reidel

Fuà, G. (1988). 'Small-scale Industry in Rural Areas: The Italian Experience', in K. Arrow (ed.), *The Balance between Industry and Agriculture in Economic Development*, 1, London: Macmillan for the International Economic Association: 259–79

(1993). *Crescita economica: le insidie delle cifre*, Bologna, Il Mulino

Gaiha, R. (1987). 'Impoverishment, Technology and Growth in Rural India', *Cambridge Journal of Economics*, 11: 23–46

Garegnani, P. (1966). 'Switching of Techniques', *Quarterly Journal of Economics*, 80: 554–67

Giusti, F. (1996). Sostituibilità dinamica capitale-lavoro. Sintesi e ampliamento di una ricerca sull'industria italiana', *Rivista italiana di demografia, economia e statistica*, 49: 1–27

Greenspan, A. (2000). 'Tecnologia ed economia', *Rivista di politica economica*, January

Grilli, E. (1994). *Interdipendenze Macroeconomiche Nord–Sud – I paesi in via di sviluppo nell'economia mondiale*, Bologna: Il Mulino

(1999). *Prospettive sullo sviluppo economico dei paesi emergenti*, Arezzo: Banca Popolare dell'Etruria e del Lazio

Grilli, E. and Zanalda, G. (1999). 'Growth and Employment in Developing Countries: Where Do We Stand?', in G. Barba Navaretti, R. Faini and G. Zanalda (eds.), *Labour Markets, Poverty, and Development*, Oxford: Clarendon Press

Habbakuk, H.J. (1967). *American and British Technology in the Nineteenth Century*, Cambridge: Cambridge University Press

Harcourt, G. (1972). *Some Cambridge Controversies in the Theory of Capital*, Cambridge: Cambridge University Press

Harrod, R. (1942). *Towards a Dynamic Economics*, London: Macmillan

Hicks, J. (1932). *The Theory of Wages*, London: Macmillan

Hoffman, W.G. (1958). *The Growth of Industrial Economy*, Manchester: Manchester University Press

International Monetary Fund (1997). *World Economic Outlook*, May

Jossa, B. (ed.) (1973). *Economia del sottosviluppo*, Bologna: Il Mulino

Kalecki, M. (1971 [1938]). 'The Determinants of the Distribution of National Income', reprinted in M. Kalecki, *Selected Essays on the Dynamics of the Capitalist Economy*, Cambridge: Cambridge University Press

Kannan, K.P. (1995). 'Public Intervention and Poverty Alleviation: A Study of the Declining Incidence of Rural Poverty in Kerala, India', *Development and Change*, 26: 701–27

(1936). *The General Theory of Employment, Interest and Money*, London: Macmillan

(1939). 'Relative Movements of Real Wages and Output', *Economic Journal*, 49: 35–51

Keynes, J.M. (1970 [1930]). *Essays in Persuasion*, London: Macmillan

Krugman, P. (1991). *Geography and Trade*, Cambridge MA: MIT Press

Kuznets, S. (1965). *Economic Growth and Structure*, New York: Norton

Lall, S. (1998). 'Exports of Manufactures by Developing Countries: Emerging Patterns of Trade and Location', *Oxford Review of Economic Policy*, 14: 54–73

Levhari, D. (1965). 'A Nonsubstitution Theorem and Switching of Techniques', *Quarterly Journal of Economics*, 79: 98–105

Lewis, A.A. (1954). 'Economic Development with Unlimited Supply of Labour', *Manchester School*, 22: 139–91

Livi Bacci, M. (1977). *A History of Italian Fertility during the Last Two Centuries*, Princeton: Princeton University Press

(1996). 'Popolazione', *Enciclopedia delle scienze sociali*, VI, Rome: Istituto della Enciclopedia Italiana

Lucas, R. (1988). 'On the Mechanics of Economic Development', *Journal of Monetary Economics*, 22: 3–42

Maddison, A. (1998). 'The Nature and Functioning of European Capitalism: A Historical and Comparative Perspective', *Banca Nazionale del Lavoro Quarterly Review*, 50: 431–80

Malthus, T.R. (1926 [1803]). *An Essay on the Principle of Population*, London; Macmillan

Marshall, A. (1949 [1890]). *Principles of Economics*, London: Macmillan

Martin, K. and Thackeray, F.G. (1948). 'The Terms of Trade of Selected Countries, 1870–1938', *Bulletin of the Oxford Institute of Statistics*, November

Marx, K. (1977). *Capital*, 3 vols, reprint edn., Moscow: Progress Publishers (orig. edn., 1st vol. 1867)

Marx, K. and Engels, F. (1959 [1848]). *Manifesto of the Communist Party*, reprinted in L.S. Feur (ed.), *Marx and Engels*, New York: Doubleday

Mendershausen, H. (1938). 'On the Significance of Professor Douglas's Production Function', *Econometrica*, 6: 143–53

Modigliani, F. (1975). 'The Life Cycle Hypothesis of Saving Twenty Years Later', in M. Parkin (ed.), *Contemporary Issues in Economics*, Manchester: Manchester University Press

Modigliani, F. *et al.* (1998). 'An Economists' Manifesto on Unemployment in the European Union', *Banca Nazionale del Lavoro Quarterly Review*, 51: 327–61

Momigliano, F. and Siniscalco, D. (1982). 'The Growth of Service Employment: A Reappraisal', *Banca Nazionale del Lavoro Quarterly Review*, 35: 269–301

Pasinetti, L.L. (1966). 'Changes in the Rate of Profit and Switches of Techniques', *Quarterly Journal of Economics*, 80: 503–17 (based on a paper presented at the Conference of the Econometric Society, Rome, September 1965)

   (1981). *Structural Change and Economic Dynamics: A Theoretical Essay on the Dynamics of the Wealth of Nations*, Cambridge: Cambridge University Press

   (2000). 'Critica della teoria neoclassica della crescita e della distribuzione', *Moneta e credito*, 54, 187–232

Phelps Brown, E.H. (1957). 'The Meaning of the Fitted Cobb–Douglas Function', *Quarterly Journal of Economics*, 71: 546–60

Piore, M. and Sabel, C.S. (1984). *The New Industrial Divide*, New York: Basic Books

Quadrio Curzio, A. (1999). 'Globalizzazione: profili economici', *Atti della Accademia Nazionale dei Lincei*, serie 9, vol. 10: 297–321

Rebelo, S. (1991). 'Long-run Policy Analysis and Long-run Growth', *Journal of Political Economy*, 99: 500–21

Ricardo, D. (1951 [1821]). *On the Principles of Political Economy*, ed. P. Sraffa, Cambridge: Cambridge University Press

Romer, P.M. (1987). 'Crazy Explanations for the Productivity Slowdown', *Macroeconomic Annual*, National Bureau of Economic Research, Cambridge MA.: MIT Press

Rothbarth, E. (1946). 'Causes of the Superior Efficiency of USA Industry Compared with British Industry', *Economic Journal*, 56: 383–90.

Samuelson, P. (1966). 'A Summing Up' (*On Paradoxes in Capital Theory: A Symposium*). *Quarterly Journal of Economics*, 80: 568–83.

Schumpeter, J.A. (1934 [1911]). *The Theory of Economic Development*, Cambridge MA: Harvard University Press

(1939). *Business Cycles – A Theoretical, Historical, and Statistical Analysis of the Capitalist Process*, New York: McGraw-Hill

(1954). *History of Economic Analysis*, London: Allen & Unwin

Sen, A. (1984). *Resources, Values and Development*, Oxford: Blackwell

Smith, A. (1961 [1776]). *An Inquiry into the Nature and Causes of the Wealth of Nations*, London: Methuen

(1976 [1759]). *The Theory of Moral Sentiments*, eds. D.D. Raphael and A.L. Macfie, Oxford: Clarendon Press

(1978). *Lectures on Jurisprudence*, eds. R.L. Meek, P.G. Stein and D.D. Raphael, Oxford: Clarendon Press

(1983). *Lectures on Rethoric and Belles Lettres*, eds. J. C. Bryce, Oxford: Clarendon Press

Solow, R. (1956). 'A Contribution to the Theory of Economic Growth', *Quarterly Journal of Economics*, 70: 65–95

(2000). 'La teoria neoclassica della crescita e della distribuzione', *Moneta e credito*, 54: 149–85

Sraffa, P. (1926). 'The Laws of Returns under Competitive Conditions', *Economic Journal*, 36: 535–50

(1960). *Production of Commodities by Means of Commodities – Prelude to a Critique of Economic Theory*, Cambridge: Cambridge University Press

Streeten, P.P. (1995). *Thinking about Development*, Cambridge: Cambridge University Press

Sylos Labini, P. (1964). 'Precarious Employment in Sicily', *International Labour Review*, March

(1969 [1956]). *Oligopoly and Technical Progress*, Cambridge MA: Harvard University Press

(1974). 'Progresso tecnico, società, diritto', in G. Guarino (ed.), *Studi in onore di G. Chiarelli*, Milan: Giuffrè

(1979). 'Prices and Income Distribution in Manufacturing Industry', reprinted in P. Sylos Labini, *The Forces of*

Economic Growth and Decline, Cambridge MA: MIT Press (1984)

(1981). 'Technological Change under Comtemporary Conditions', reprinted in P. Sylos Labini, *The Forces of Economic Growth and Decline*, Cambridge, MA: MIT Press (1984)

(1983a). Il *sottosviluppo e l'economia contemporanea*, Roma–Bari: Laterza (Spanish edn., *Subdesarollo y Economía Contemporánea*, Barcelona: Editorial Critica, 1984)

(1983b). 'Factors Affecting Changes in Productivity', reprinted in P. Sylos Labini, *The Forces of Economic Growth and Decline*, Cambridge, MA: MIT Press (1984)

(1984). *The Forces of Economic Growth and Decline*, Cambridge, MA: MIT Press.

(1988). 'The Great Debates on the Laws on Returns and the Value of Capital: When Will Economists Finally Accept their Own Logic?', reprinted in P. Sylos Labini, *Economic Growth and Business Cycles – Prices and the Process of Cyclical Development*, Aldershot: Edward Elgar (1993)

(1990). 'Technical Progress, Unemployment and Economic Dynamics', reprinted in P. Sylos Labini, *Economic Growth and Business Cycles – Prices and the Process of Cyclical Development*, Aldershot, Edward Elgar (1993)

(1991). 'Development Planning in India', in *Discussion Papers*, 1, Dipartimento di economia pubblica, Università di Roma 'La Sapienza'

(1992a). ' "Capitalism, Socialism and Democracy" and Large-scale Firms', reprinted in P. Sylos Labini, *Economic Growth and Business Cycles – Prices and the Process of Cyclical Development*, Aldershot: Edward Elgar (1993)

(1992b). 'Reflections on the Constitution of an International Research Center Connected with the United Nations', paper presented at the 5th International Amaldi Conference, Heidelberg, July (the proceedings are available at the Accademia Nazionale dei Lincei, Roma)

(1993a). *Terzo mondo: varietà di percorsi*, Rome: Accademia Nazionale dei Lincei

(1993b). 'Long-run changes in the Wage and Price Mechanisms

and the Process of Growth', reprinted in P. Sylos Labini, *Economic Growth and Business Cycles – Prices and the Process of Cyclical Development*, Aldershot: Edward Elgar (1993)

(1995a). 'Carlo Marx: è tempo di un bilancio' and 'Riflessioni conclusive', first and last chapter of the book, *Carlo Marx: È tempo di un bilancio* (preface by Giacomo Becattini), Rome–Bari: Laterza (1994)

(1995b). 'Why the Interpretation of the Cobb–Douglas Production Function must be Radically Changed', *Structural Change and Economic Dynamics*, 6: 485–504

(1999). 'The Employment Issue: Investment, Flexibility and the Competition of Developing Countries', *Banca Nazionale del Lavoro Quarterly Review*, 52

Sylos Labini, S. (1997). 'I rappporti tra base monetaria, crescita economica e prezzi in Italia nel periodo 1970–96', *Sassari: Quaderni di economia a finanza*, Banco di Sardegna

Temple, J. (1999). 'The New Growth Evidence', *Journal of Economic Literature*, March: 112–56

Tocqueville, A. de (1951). *De la démocratie en Amerique*, Paris: Genin

United Nations Conference on Trade and Development (UNCTAD) (1999). *Handbook of International Trade and Development Statistics, 1996–7*, Geneva and New York: United Nations

United Nations Development Programme (various years). *Human Development Report*, New York: United Nations

Various authors (1997), *Le livre noir du communisme*, Paris: Laffont

Volpi, F. (1994). *Introduzione all'economia dello sviluppo*, Milan: Franco Angeli

Wicksell, K. (1934 [1901–6]). *Lectures on Political Economy*, London: Routledge

Wood, A. (1994). *North–South Trade, Employment and Inequality – Changing Fortunes in a Skill-Driven World*, Oxford: Clarendon Press

World Bank (1993). *Women's Education in Developing Countries – Barriers, Benefits, and Policies*, eds. E.M. King and M. Anne Hill, Baltimore and London: Johns Hopkins University Press

(various years) *World Development Report*, New York: Oxford University Press

Yunus, M. (1997). *Vers un monde sans pauvreté*, Paris: Lats

Zagler, M. (1999). *Endogenous Growth, Market Failures and Economic Policy*, London: Macmillan

Index